A Dinner Date with The Mad Duck

Princess Umul Hatiyya Ibrahim Mahama

A Dinner Date with the Mad Duck © 2015
Princess Umul Hatiyya Ibrahim Mahama

ISBN-13: 978-1517301224
ISBN-10: 151730122X

Contact the author via
info@themadduckcompany.com

Published by:
The Mad Duck Company
P. O. Box TF368
Trade Fair
Accra - Ghana

Printed in Ghana.

Lord, I thank you for bequeathing me with the gift of writing. My life would be incomplete without this gift.

And to all my fans, thank you very much for reading all that I write. This book is dedicated to you, your good travels in body and spirit, and your peace of mind.

TABLE OF CONTENTS

Introduction   7

SECTION 1

Chapter One: My Mystery Client   11
Chapter Two: The Value of Pain   39
Chapter Three: The Power of Learning   65
Chapter Four: Wake Up Sleeping Giant   69
Chapter Five: Courage, A Winners Best Friend   77
Chapter Six: Woman You Are An Agent of Change   81
Chapter Seven: Take the Bull by the Horns   91

SECTION 2

Photos to Reflect Upon and Inspire   105

SECTION 3

Chapter Eight: Rock the Boat At All Cost   115
Chapter Nine: Lead by Example   137
Chapter Ten: A Woman Is Like A Teabag   147
Chapter Eleven: Who Will Mourn When You Are Gone   155

About the Author   163

INTRODUCTION

Can a conversation make the difference between a life gone one way and not another? It can when it's an extraordinary series of discussions between people who are open to clearly looking at their lives and how to take them to the deepest levels, no matter the hardships. A Dinner Date with The Mad Duck is the record of an intense, probing and ultimately life-transforming conversation between two people over an extended period of time.

In 2007, Abdul Aziz Dinnani meets by sheer circumstance the man who becomes his mentor, accomplished surgeon Alex Bond. Prior to their meeting, Abdul was a classic lost soul. He becomes Alex's driver at a time when Alex's own life is deeply stressed. In a series of riveting exchanges, the two passionately discuss the things that matter most: how we spend our time, how to make meaning of our lives, and who and how we love.

The give and take between the two covers healthy and crippling life choices, the influences of esteemed historical figures, contemporary works of nonfiction and fiction, and personal philosophies. But in essence, it covers the things that matter most: how to do the best with our lives on this planet.

The book is divided into two sections: Abdul before his life is completely changed by Alex's guidance, and Abdul, years later, after he has found fulfillment. And that fulfillment has a lot to do with helping others, which is a key life lesson.

My role in this work is a sounding board for Abdul's journey, from knowing him as a very young man to discovering and discussing his tremendous changes and successes, and the sources of those changes.

The book also presents you with a selection of photos from my travels around the world. These tie into the book's journeys, mental and physical, for all the parties involved. For me, travel is the most fulfilling, life-expanding mission I have undertaken. When you travel, you see humanity in all its glory and its travail. Your barriers drop, and you can connect. This book is all about human connection, and I hope its lessons bring you to a higher place.

SECTION 1

SECTION 1

CHAPTER ONE

My Mystery Client

"The key is to keep company only with people who uplift you, whose presence calls forth your best."

— Epictetus

I just read in the *Accra Tribune* that Abdul Aziz Dinnani and Partners are setting up a law practice here in Accra. Is this the Abdul I know?

Abdul was a very good friend of mine. We lived in the same neighborhood and attended the same secondary school. Abdul was one of the most sagacious guys I had ever known. In school, while I struggled with math and science, Abdul would consistently score very high marks.

To top it all, he was also good-looking and came from an estimable home. Abdul was popular and liked, as well as a kind-hearted person. Everyone's world lit up when Abdul was around. He was the lifeblood of any party, and because he genuinely loved and cared for others, he was always invited to gatherings, educational shows, and quizzes. As a result, his handsomeness, high IQ and convivial nature attracted droves of people into his presence. Abdul was also an entertainment prefect and liked to dazzle the students every Saturday night with a variety of entertainment shows. He organized rap concerts, eating competitions, fun fairs and the premier jazz festival ever held in the school.

We all wondered how he hatched the idea of holding a jazz festival—somehow Abdul was ahead of his peers in this and many ways. Though he was only 17 years old, Abdul was the man most women dreamt of settling down with because he generally treated women with love and respect. Because of his sweet nature, his female friends in particular would constantly clamor for his attention. As a 14-year-old, I loved and appreciated Abdul as a friend. He challenged me to study hard and to be open hearted. Judging from what you saw, you could predict that Abdul would be an influential person in the future. He had both high IQ and EQ (emotional quotient), and all that makes a person successful.

When he finished secondary school, Abdul moved from our neighborhood; he left for University in Manchester. We were all so happy for him. I had no doubt that Abdul would shine at University. But before the move, all his friends decided to give him a surprise going-away party. The plan was that I would invite him to my house, where about 20 of his friends would secretly congregate and spring the surprise on him.

Abdul loved food, so after he arrived and we chatted for a little while, his question was about food. "Where is the food you promised to cook for me," he asked? I told him the *table of Waakye* (which is a dish of rice and beans) and grilled chicken was neatly laid in the next room so we moved in there to eat. On opening the door, the whole room reverberated with *Surprise!!!* He was shocked and wanted to run out of the room. What? *Kofi, Nana Yaa, Moses,*

Zuwera, Fahima, when did you plan this? All he kept saying after that was, *"Oh my goodness, I can't believe this."* After about 30 minutes he calmed down and went to the table to take his food. But this time around it wasn't a heap, it was a tiny portion. Abdul was in a state of bewilderment. There was joy and laughter in the room. Every one of us gave a farewell speech.

At various times we all shed tears—we were overwhelmed with emotions, which was something to see. The parting was the hardest for me. I cried until my eyes were sore. I wished him well—I knew without a shadow of doubt that he would thrive in Manchester. When he arrived there, he called to let me know. Over time, we continued to stay in touch, but the distance inevitably confined our friendship. We would write letters and call when we were on holidays, but our friendship was just not the same. I missed my times with Abdul and even though I tried to make new friends, there was no one quite like him.

In his calls, he said things were different, though he was homesick and missed us all. I told him it was because he was in a new environment and that in a few weeks he would make new friends and adjust to his new life. I got on with school and continued to write him letters. From his replies you could tell he was settling in well. He always mentioned a friend Douglas, and on occasions I got to speak to this friend on the phone.

From the outset, I thought Douglas was a good friend to Abdul, but whenever I spoke to Douglas and asked how school was going he would say, "Fine, but half of the time I am not in class because I have been partying all night and I am too tired in the morning to go for lectures." Then I asked Abdul if he was attending lectures and not partying with Douglas and he always answered in the affirmative.

However as the months rolled by, I heard from another university friend that Abdul was getting into trouble with the authorities and recently had been in trouble with the police for drunk driving. I couldn't believe my ears. Abdul? I called him and we talked as usual, not giving him a clue that I was aware of his new lifestyle. I then asked him if he was regularly partying with Douglas and he admitted that he was.

What had come over Abdul? How could he throw his future away by emulating a person whom he just met? I would spend nights asking God to let Abdul see the destruction he would ultimately bring upon himself. Well, correspondence from Abdul over time became scantier and scantier until it stopped coming altogether. I tried calling him on several occasions, but he simply wouldn't answer my calls. I continued writing for about one year without success, so I gave up.

During my late teenage and early adult years, different people told me that Abdul dropped out of university and was living rough. He was seen in Birmingham, Liverpool, and later on in London. Things got so bad that his parents didn't even know where he was. From time to time I wondered where he was and what he was doing with his life. Abdul simply disappeared.

After reading about this law firm establishing a branch in Accra, I immediately called Dinnani and Partners, to find out if it was the same Abdul I knew. I was told he was currently in London for a meeting. I left my details and I knew that he would surely return my call when he received the message.

During the day, I kept stealing glances at my phone just to make sure I hadn't missed a call from Abdul. I hoped I could catch him in London as I was also leaving on that Friday. Around 6pm my phone rang.

Hello, is this Princess?
Yes it is. Who is this please?
It is Abdul Aziz.
Wow, it's great to hear from you.
Where have you been Abdul?
Where have you been yourself, Princess?

After chatting for about 10 minutes, we agreed to meet that weekend at my favourite Chinese restaurant, *Wong Kei* on Wardour Street in Soho. I choose this venue because I knew that Abdul was a foodie. Wong Kei is a plain-looking restaurant, but the food there is one of the best I have eaten outside Beijing. I kept wondering: was he still the captivating and passionate person I knew? I couldn't wait for the weekend to discover all these things. Finally, the weekend came and I headed for *Wong Kei*.

Abdul was actually waiting for me. Immediately he saw me, and he opened his arms to embrace me. He gave me one of the warmest hugs I had received in a long while. We were locked in this embrace for a while, and only realized how long we had been hugging by the stares I received from other diners. After our long hug, we sat down and I called the waiter and began to order. As I couldn't wait anymore to have my curiosity satisfied I got right into the conversation.

"So where have you been all this while?" I asked.

"Princess, it is a very long story, but I know with you I can't leave anything out. I have to give you all the details, the pleasant and the not-so-pleasant ones too. Well, when I left Accra in 1991 for Manchester, I met Douglas. You remember that friend of mine, don't you?"

"Yes I do."

"Well, meeting him was the worst event that ever happened to me, but actually it all worked out for my good in the end. I missed home very much when I first arrived in Manchester; I was lonely and didn't have anyone to call a friend. So when Douglas—who masked as a friend—came around, I opened up to him. He would invite me to go clubbing with him. Initially I declined, since clubbing wasn't my sort of thing, but after a while I couldn't brush off his offers because I needed someone to talk to and spend time with, and he was the most affable course mate. Douglas made me feel like a human being. He would check up on me constantly and seemed to care—or so I thought at the time. Going to Manchester made me realize how loved I was while in Ghana.

"Now looking back at Ghana, I know I was fortunate to have been in such a loving environment. I remember even in the days things were rough for my dad and mum, family and friends just filled our home with love, friendship and joy so we children didn't feel the difficulty that much. Yes, we no longer ate large chunks of meat or drank milk and sometimes had to scrounge for food, but it didn't make a difference in how we loved and treated each other.

"So now back to Douglas. I started hanging out with Douglas and he introduced me to alcohol. Initially I drank very little, so I would be able to attend lectures after partying during the week. But Douglas somehow had a subtle way of influencing me so our partying grew from twice a week to four days a week, and my alcohol intake grew with it.

"After a while I realized that I couldn't live a day without drinking. Somehow I enjoyed the false sense of pleasure alcohol brought me. The alcohol numbed my pain of missing home. I really missed my family and wanted to return to Ghana. In actual fact I should have told my parents exactly how things were and I believe they would have done everything possible to remedy the situation, even if it meant returning to Ghana and they losing the yearly fees they had paid. My parents loved me that much. I recall once when my grades started to drop they were concerned and flew out to Manchester to see if all was well.

"During the week they visited, I was sober and put on perfect behavior, so they didn't suspect anything sinister. I promised them to work hard and improve my grades. Little did they know that the reason my grades were falling was because I was no longer studying. I was just partying. They expected things to improve the next semester like I had promised them, but unfortunately things never did, all because I was still spending my waking minutes with Douglas. Things got so bad that during one semester, I partied every single day of the week, so I never stepped into a class. I only went to write exams, and of course never being in class meant that I failed miserably.

"At this point I realized things were rotten, but guess what? I didn't make any drastic changes to turn my life around for the better. I still didn't get Douglas out of my life. Finally, since I wasn't participating in school and had failed three semesters, I was expelled. 1993 was the darkest period in my life. Even though I was deflated and depressed, I still hid everything from my parents. I moved off campus and rented a room in town, and then I got a job in the local McDonalds. During those burdensome days, I would think of you, Princess. On many occasions I was tempted to call you, but I didn't because I was ashamed of what I had become. I just couldn't gather the courage, or maybe I was too proud and didn't feel worthy of your love and the love of my family. I felt I had let my parents down. How stupid I was.

"Looking back now, I can see I should have ignored those voices in my head. The voices that kept on telling me that you all would reject me. So with this pain, I drowned myself in work. My work ethos actually earned me a few prizes. I won the hardest-worker award for our branch, then for the area, then Manchester, and the big one was for the entire North. Even though I was working hard, I was miserable inside because I had abandoned all my dreams. My work was out of sync with who I really was. There were days after work when my mind would drift to the dreams I had as a youth. The days I was confident that I would become the next Albert Einstein, propounding new theories in physics or the next Mandela who will liberate his people from oppression. Believe me, those youthful years were my happiest. However I had abandoned my dreams because of the poor quality of people I associated with."

"Abdul," I interjected, "You have made a very profound statement. You truly do become like the people you spend your time with. If you spend time with people going nowhere, you will end up going nowhere. The Bible rightly puts it this way: *"Bad character corrupts good company."* However, if you spend your time with go-getters you will start to think and act like one. Just reading about the achievements of a heavy hitter urges you to achieve great things too."

"Princess, your mention of reading reminds me of the days we used to lend each other books and compete over how many books we could read in a month. Many times, because I wanted to win that race, I would read late into the night, sometimes not sleeping until 4am. Autobiographies were my favourite. I was always inspired after reading one. I still remember how I felt after reading *The Autobiography of Martin Luther King, Jr.* That book made me laugh and cry, but ultimately it made me think. It also got me exasperated; not in a way where I wanted to exact retribution on those who passed the laws of segregation and other laws which marginalized people of colour, but angry at injustice. I remember resolving to make a difference in the areas in which I felt I was planted—in math, science and politics.

"Until I read his book, I hadn't the faintest idea that Martin Luther King was actually a Baptist minister. I knew he was a civil rights activist, but I somehow thought he was a lawyer. Dr. King was certainly a person who defied the establishment. In this 21st century if a preacher was actively involved in politics or running for political office, he would be labeled all sorts of names. I can imagine what his congregation would say. The reaction of his congregation would be, 'If you are called by God to preach the gospel, remain in the pulpit, because you can't mix religion and politics.' That preacher would be persecuted and would likely lose the support of his congregation. This example shows how we humans sometimes misunderstand God and even misrepresent him. Another thing that struck me a great deal about Dr. King was his ability to love and forgive his oppressors. His capacity to love and forgive, as well as all of his convictions clearly showed he had a divine mandate to do what he did.

"The speech he gave on 3rd April 1968 to the congregation of Mason Temple in Memphis Tennessee, where he spoke about having 'been to the mountain top' is a speech that still gives me goosebumps. He said, *'Well, I don't know what will happen now. We have got some difficult days ahead … But I'm not concerned about that now. I just want to do God's will. And He's allowed me to go up the mountain. And I've looked over. And I've seen the Promised Land. I may not get there with you. But I want you to know tonight, that we as a people, will get to the Promised Land. And so I'm happy tonight. I'm not worried about anything. I'm not fearing any man! Mine eyes have seen the glory of the coming of the Lord.'* Wow, what knowledge!"

"Abdul, you recounting this story really brings back memories of my visit to the Lincoln Memorial in Washington DC. Standing at the exact spot where the famous *I Have a Dream* speech was made—that for me was a dream come true."

"Princess, I also look forward to experiencing that surreal moment one day. Now where was I before drifting off into Dr. King?"

"You were talking about reading."

"Oh yes, please forgive me. As I was saying, because I used to read in those days, I was inspired and challenged to be all that I was created to be. I realized however, that once I threw away my reading habit, my level of inspiration and my passion also went out of the window.

"However, I can tell you that every now and again an angel in human form was sent to help me see the light, but somehow I still wouldn't budge. I remember a colleague of mine, David, when I worked at McDonalds; this was in 1997. David was different. He was energetic, positive, and always talked about changing the world. At lunchtime, we'd find him reading and not a part of the mindless discussions me and the other guys would be having in the canteen. At times we would deliberately make so much noise to distract him, but he never budged. David was focused. His focus reminded me of who I used to be and this intimidated me and made me unkind to him. On one occasion we made so much noise arguing about Manchester United and Chelsea (as if we were coaches or owners of the club) that he couldn't read and simply left the room.

"There was something about David; he was kind and forgiving. After that incident you would have thought that he would have been angry with us. But he wasn't. Yes, looking back now, David was an angel sent to me but I didn't acknowledge it. After working in McDonalds for 10 years, I got bored and left. I was unemployed for eight months because I was looking not just for a job to pay my bills, but a job that would satisfy me and enable me fully use my talents.

"One day in March 2004, a friend I had known for many years called me out the blue. We chatted about life and my next career move. After speaking to him, he persuaded me to take up a temporary job as a minicab driver while I figured out what I wanted to do. I enjoyed driving so I knew that I would enjoy being a cabbie. I immediately applied for a Private Hire Vehicle Drivers License. When my license arrived, I registered unhesitantly with Excellent Cabs in Stratford London E7. My first day at work was fun: I was assigned to a colleague who trained me for a week and I went on all his calls with him. For the first time in a very long while, I felt alive. For me, the best part of my job was meeting different people and helping them get to their destinations. Because I was happy, I worked very hard.

"Within a year, as a result of my dedication, I was moved to our city branch on Fleet Street, London EC1. Here I was driving business executives, CEOs, celebrities, lawyers, doctors and people making waves. This job opened my eyes to a world of possibilities. I began to dream again. Dreaming was a habit I stopped engaging in many years prior. But driving movers and shakers in the city somehow turned it on. Every day I would go home excited looking forward to sharing my dreams, thoughts and ideas with my friends. But all I got in return was a cold shoulder and an attitude that basically said, 'Get real young man, your dreams are pure science fiction.'

"I would get upset and even cry sometimes because I wondered why people I loved and cared for deeply would denigrate my dreams. By this point I was married to Halima and had two girls, three-year-old Zeneida, and two-year-old Maltiti. Though I shared with Halima what I was observing in the city and my feelings about it, she most often didn't show any interest. This broke my heart."

"Abdul," I interjected, "You know what? You shouldn't fault loved ones and friends when they are not interested in your dreams. People can only give you what they have. If a person is a dreamer, they can understand and will be interested in another person's dreams. But if you are not a dreamer, you may tend to see dreamers as lunatics, people who are not real. Also, most people are afraid of dreamers. If they are your loved ones, they know the price they may have to pay to support you, the dreamer, so they will do anything to talk you out of it.

"Some people love the safety and comfort of their lives— even if they are discontented, they would rather remain dispirited than rock the boat. What they forget is that real life is lived on the wire. Life is best enjoyed when risk, discomfort, positive stress, challenges, pain, passion, energy, and joy are the order of the day," I said.

"I get it now Princess. If I knew this at that time, I wouldn't have been enraged at them. The mistake I made was that I sought validation and endorsement from my loved ones. Since I didn't have friends who were dreamers, I drowned my sorrows with work, spending less and less time at home. Of course this behavior wreaked havoc in my relationship with Halima. I consoled myself that work was going so well. However, the truth was that the bickering and tension at home affected me badly. I was unhappy."

"Abdul, you should have made new friends. You should have sought out people who were like-minded and could understand your dreams. You should have also understood Halima's frustrations. She felt alienated, and your absence from home also depleted her energy because she was saddled with the demands of raising the children. She felt like a single parent, since she was doing the school runs, attending the parent evenings, and going to parties all alone. On most days she also didn't have any adult conversations. She only heard 'children talk,' which can be frustrating."

"I understand now, Princess. During this crucial period in my life, I was sent another angel. And this is where my real life started to unfold.

"I met Alex one wintery Wednesday evening in December 2007. I was called to pick him up at The Royal Courts of Justice, on the Strand in WC2. Alex was a neurosurgeon with St. Thomas

Hospital. He was in court because he had been accused of committing an error during an operation on a famous rock star, who then died. As this was a trial involving a celebrity, it was highly publicized. It was in the news, in the papers, on the radio and on the Internet.

"When he got in the car, he smiled and greeted me. I couldn't believe a man under intense pressure could even smile, much less acknowledge me. While I was waiting to pick him up, the media crowded around like hungry lions ready to pounce on a prey. I counted over 30 media representatives, all holding cameras and waiting for Alex to emerge from the courtroom.

"I asked Alex how his day was going and to my surprise he said, 'Well, thanks.' Wow, I thought, was he on some form of medication or something? How could a person be doing well under such strenuous circumstances? The ride back to St. Thomas seemed very short for me because we were engaged in conversation. I thought I was privileged to have met him."

"Abdul, would you mind picking me up every day for the court appearances until this trial is over?" he asked.

"I could hardly believe it. I calmly said, 'I will be honoured to do that, sir.'"

"See you at 9am tomorrow and have a good evening," he said.

"I couldn't stop smiling after Alex left. Wow, what great fortune! I really felt that I had struck gold because of what I knew I could learn and become by spending time with Alex. A person who had achieved so much—I felt he could teach me a thing or two about success. I couldn't wait to share this piece of great news with Halima. When I got home I described my promising fortune, but received only a grunt and an ok from Halima. I was crushed.

"How could anyone not see the significance of being the driver of one of the world's leading neurosurgeons? Alex Bond is a man who successfully operates on over 300 patients a year. A man pioneering groundbreaking brain surgeries and who had invented surgical instruments. He had received countless awards, including a knighthood by the Queen. I couldn't wait to pick him up in the morning. After having a bowl of delicious vegetable soup prepared by Halima, I went to bed.

"I woke up the next day in very high spirits, excited about my day with Alex. Since I was picking him up at 9am, I decided to start my day at 6am and not the usual 8am. I wanted to use the time to research the trial. I needed to know the facts for myself and not the facts the media were promulgating. At exactly 8:45am I parked outside St. Thomas Hospital, and called to let him know that I was outside. He came down immediately. I opened the door for him and took his briefcase. I'll recount our conversations as best I recall them.

"Good morning, Sir."

"Good morning Abdul, and how are you today?"

"I am very well thanks, and you Sir?"

"I am fabulous and looking forward to the great things in store for me today."

"Great things"? I thought to myself. You are going to court to be grilled, quizzed and battered and you call those great things in store for you?

And then Alex began to speak again.

"Words either give life or death. So it is entirely up to you what you want your words to give. Life or death. That's why deliberately choosing to speak only words that give life is a sure way of emerging out of any dark hole you may find yourself in. I know my response to your greeting may have startled you. With the kind of pressure I am under, you may have been expecting me to speak the language of a victim. You know what I have come to learn? I have come to understand that our thoughts create our words. Our words create our moods, our moods then dictate our actions. And our actions create our experience or our life. So what you choose to think about and what you say are very important."

"You are right, Alex: I remember reading the classic *Think and Grow Rich* by Napoleon Hill, and wondering how anyone can think and actually become rich. However this explanation you have given makes perfect sense."

"Abdul, what you say becomes your reality. I expect great things to happen to me today; that's what I expect and so that is what I will continually say. Just think about my meeting you yesterday: I told myself that I was looking forward to great things happening to me, and I met you. My passion, apart from performing surgeries, is to teach people to become all they were meant to be. Yesterday when we spoke, you certainly struck me as a man seeking change. So I am willing to share all that I know with you in whatever time we have to spend together.

"This morning, I spent an hour thinking deeply about my goals and my purpose in life. This simple act, known as *visualization*, will change your life if you practice it daily. I thought about the commissioning of a world-class neurology center I intend to build in Antananarivo, in Madagascar. Once it is built, I will work there for 12 weeks a year and offer free surgeries to people who cannot afford them or who would die otherwise. I thought about three instruments I am inventing, for which I'm working on patents. I also thought about the love my family has for me. Finally I dwelt on the success of my students. I imagined a 100% pass rate for them.

"Because I spent this hour visualizing my goals, I am saturated with my dreams—the challenges of today cannot hem me in. Visualization also reminds me of what is important to me in the grand scheme of life. And because I am innocent, why should I panic? Why should I approach each day with trepidation? I will be exonerated, so it is very important that I remain focused on *what is true, what is pure, what is lovely, and what is admirable.*"

We arrived at the courts in no time and I wished I had more miles to go with Alex.

"Thank you very much Alex for all you have taught me this morning. I am eternally grateful."

"My pleasure, Abdul. Have a terrific day, and may your day be filled with goodness and favour. Do pick me up at 4pm."

When I dropped Alex off, I was called to take a client from Oxford Street to Chelsea. Because I had been with Alex, I noticed that his gracefulness and radiance was rubbing off on me. Somehow I started emulating Alex. I smiled and greeted my client. She was the lead actress in the West End production *The Phantom of the Opera*. While driving, my mind kept drifting to the conversations I had with Alex. How I wish I lived in the same house with him! At exactly 3:45pm I was parked outside the courts.

Alex said, "You have the pleasure of driving me home today, Abdul."

"Where is home?" I asked.

"Guildford in Surrey, in the South East of England. I usually work in the hospital from Monday to Thursday. Fridays are my days of learning, researching, thinking and strategizing. On Fridays, I also catch up on new neurological developments from my peers around the world. After you drop me off, in the next hour my recharging session begins."

"Recharging session? How do you recharge?"

"Upon arriving home, after receiving hugs from the quads (that's what I call my children) and my wife Jean, I move to the bathroom to have a warm shower or bath. As our bodies constitute about 60% water, water is not only beneficial, it is essential to our survival. Now what a shower does for me is that it recharges the body so I can focus on the conversation and activities I will engage in that night. I never miss my bath ritual when I get home in the evening.

"Now Abdul, you may be thinking: take a shower even in winter? When the weather is below freezing? I recall a time I was in Novosibirsk in Russia in the freezing month of January. Novosibirsk is sometimes referred to as the capital of Siberia. There, temperatures can be as cold as - 46 degrees Celsius. It is the coldest place I have ever been, but even when I was there, I never failed to practice this ritual. What happens is that when you take a hot shower at the end of the day, you feel warm no matter the outside temperature. You will also feel refreshed. Can you imagine how a fish feels when it is out of water? After a shower, I then take a glass or two of water to flush out the toxins in my system. After this ritual, I am ready to soar. I can listen to Jean and make meaningful contributions to our conversation. Jean is an artist, so I can enjoy her stories about the paintings she may be working on.

"I can also engage better with my sons Caleb, Paul, Adrian and five-year-old Nigel. Nigel enjoys painting just like his mother. I usually sit with him and get him to entertain me with his magnificent works, which are doodlings. Another ritual I always engage in whenever I am in town is having a family dinner at 7pm daily. I never miss this unless I am working at night or out of the country. When you spend time with your family, you have the opportunity to nurture them. You can coach and guide them.

"Believe me Abdul, in this day and age, there are a lot of negative influences out there. How many times do you switch on the TV and see stories about people impacting the world positively? Even if a major news network carries such a story, it will usually be at the end of a broadcast. Most networks carry news of war, destruction and all the ills of this world. Why don't mainstream newspapers carry headlines like '40-year-old teacher grants scholarship to 5 students' or 'Man rescues village by building a hospital'? Who would rather read news about people killing one another? And do you think negative stories evoke positive emotions like courage or joy?

"Once children are affirmed and loved, the last places they will seek solutions from are the TV, the newspapers and advice columns in magazines, which most often do not promote positive values. Never forget that some media houses are in the business to make money and make money alone. And due to this, they are not concerned with screening the stories they report or thinking about the impact their stories have on others. That is the least of their worries. Due to these reasons we chose not to have a TV in our home. This saves us so much time and accords us time to bond as a family.

"After dinner, we engage in fun activities or I help the children out with their homework. We all then retire to bed at 9pm. When I get to snuggle up in bed with Jean and really talk to her is one of my favourite parts of the day. I have a policy not to sleep for more than 5 or 6 hours so usually by 3am I am awake and begin my day."

"Alex, you mean you wake up at 3am when the world is still asleep?"

"Yes, on most nights I do. We have been given 24 hours every day and come to think of it, that's not a lot of time if you have much to do. If you sleep it all away, you are simply sleeping your life away. Immediately after I wake up, I spend an hour reading, praying and meditating. I then spend 30 minutes swimming in the heated pool. I write for 30 minutes and then spend another 30 minutes with Jean having breakfast and talking. The children wake up at 5:45am and get ready for school. I wake them up, give them hugs and quick massages and leave the house at 6am. My day in the hospital starts at 7am. I spend the entire 40 minutes on the train to Waterloo Station reading and writing. I make sure that every minute of my life is accounted for. No time wasted. If I weren't sharing with you now, I would have been reading.

"You have to live your life with the consciousness that today may be your last day. You have to live with intent. You must go through life with your eyes wide open. That is the only way you will make your life count."

"Alex, I am so thankful for all you have shared with me. I can't tell you how enriched I have become since I met you. May God bless you richly."

"The pleasure is mine, Abdul. Truthfully I have enjoyed every minute with you. I believe in your gifts and talents, I believe in your dreams, so go on and be all you were created to be."

Just as we arrived in his driveway, the children ran outside. It was then that I knew that Paul, his second son (who I guessed would be around 14 years old) who came out in his wheelchair, suffered from Down Syndrome. Jean came out too and gave Alex a warm hug and kiss. I must say I was a little envious about this elaborate welcome ceremony. Looking on, you would have thought that Alex had been away for a while and just got back. Wow, how I wished my home were a place of such joy.

As if Alex could read my thoughts, he said, "One agreement we have in this house is that every member of the family is important and should be welcomed like royalty. If we were all home and Jean came back from a meeting or the supermarket, we would all come and give her a royal welcome. We do the same for the children too. What we are trying to communicate to the children is their *Value*.

Also, when you treat them this way, they want to spend more time at home because they feel wanted."

He went on: "Never forget that people will go where they are celebrated. There is no point being envious of me if you are not willing to put in the time, effort and energy it will take to get these results. All I want to add is that practicing what I am sharing with you will yield the same results, but always remember that it takes time and effort."

He opened his briefcase and paid me, and also gave me a tip. He then gave me a book by Robin Sharma titled, *Who Will Cry When You Die.*

"Read this Abdul. It's a signed copy from Robin. This book will change your life."

Alex gave me a big hug.
"See you at 9am on Monday."

Tears were rolling down my cheeks. Such love, I thought. I had met Alex only two weeks ago, so why would he give me so much? We live in a world where people don't give freely, especially to strangers. Everything about Alex was different. Driving back to London, so many thoughts were running through my head. Questions I would ask Alex, the love and kindness I would practice at home, and the new habits I would learn. With this knowledge I knew I needed time to let it all sink in so I decided to close for the day and head home to East Ham. On my way home, the traffic was heavy because of a football match between West Ham United and Arsenal at West Ham's home ground in Upton Park.

Under normal circumstances I would have been fuming, but that day was different—I felt different. I was in high spirits, and my mind was actively searching for solutions to the dilemmas I was facing at home. I was too engrossed in my thoughts to bother about the traffic. I also begun thinking about Alex and the frustrations he must face on a daily basis. I could just imagine him performing surgery on a patient and the patient dying. How hard that must be for him. However, in the midst of these challenges, he would still maintain a smile and help his children with their homework when he got home.

I made up my mind that in any situation I found myself I would ask the question, "What would Alex do?" That way I was guaranteed to remain calm and find a solution. When I got home Halima and the children were surprised to see me, as it was 7:30pm and not the usual late time I got home. I greeted them all with a smile. My eldest daughter Zeneida ran to me. I gave her a big hug.

"Daddy I have missed you!"
"I have missed you too, Zeneida, how was school today?"

And so began our conversation. After teaching Zeneida, I put both girls to bed.

Halima was not as enthusiastic, but I understood her. After years of neglect, I wouldn't expect her to show me such affection as Jean would show Alex. However, after reminding myself about what Alex said, and in order to share in the joys of a loving and caring relationship, I sincerely acted in a loving manner. I knew now that a loving relationship takes time and effort. Usually when I get home, the last thing I am thinking about is taking a shower. But after Alex's lesson on water, I found myself rushing to the bathroom to try out this new habit. After some 20 minutes, I was refreshed and really felt energetic. Drinking water was tough though. But I did drink half a glass, which was a start. This was an area I knew I needed to work on. After dinner, I settled in to read Sharma's *Who Will Cry When You Die.*

Then it was 11pm. I couldn't believe I had been reading for an hour and a half. I was just consumed by the book. Well, I had work to go to tomorrow, so I went straight to bed.

At last Monday came. I'd been counting the hours since Friday. By 8:45am, I was parked outside St. Thomas Hospital waiting for Alex.

"The court will be rather brief today," he said. "I will be engaged there for about 30 minutes while you wait for me. After that, I will spend the day giving lectures at the Royal College of Surgeons in Lincoln's Inn Fields and the Great Ormond Street Hospital. That is our agenda for the day. However Abdul, I want you to attend both lectures, as I know you will be enriched by the experience. Both lectures are about conducting successful brain surgery. However difficult, you will learn from them. Also, I will have an hour break so we can go for lunch and spend time sharing ideas. Even though I have known you for a very short time, I can say that our hearts connect. I can feel your heart and the change you desperately want in your life. I am willing to be that vessel of change. For me it will be a great honour."

"Alex, I am touched by all that you are doing for me."

"Abdul, the first principle I would like to share with you today is knowing who you are. I would say it is the foundation on which everything else will be built. Do you think I draw my value from being one of the most respected neurosurgeons in the world? Believe me, if I did, I surely would not be where I am today. I will tell you a little bit about myself now. My dad was an astute politician, and as a young boy I exhibited some speaking prowess, and I was empathetic towards people. I also enjoyed political debates. So somehow my father assumed I would follow in his footsteps. He tried to make me a politician, but I rebelled. Since I was already 18 years old, he didn't take much interest in me due to this rebellion.

"I always wanted to study medicine. I was passionate about the brain, fascinated by it since my first biology lesson. I gobbled up amazing brain facts such as, the brain consists of 100 billion neurons, it has 100,000 miles of blood vessels, and that it holds 2% of the total body weight (meaning humans have the largest brain-to-body size). Learning that our brains have the ability to expand their connections and be altered just awed me. I wanted to understand how this supercomputer worked.

"Through hard work and dedication, I passed my GCSE's A levels and gained a scholarship to University College London. Things were tough: I had to find a job and due to our heavy workload in medical school, I worked at Sainsbury's on the night shift just to feed myself. My scholarship paid for tuition only so I had to fund everything else myself. One particular day I was weary, and felt abandoned; however, I found solace in reading. I read a statement that changed my life forever. The statement was simple: *I am made in the image and likeness of God.* This statement hit me so strongly. Knowing that my identity was not from man or from anything I would ever achieve liberated me from the emotional turmoil and inferiority complex I sometimes had.

"Consider this highly publicized trial: think about how crushed I would be if my identity came from my status as one of the world's leading neurosurgeons. When the trial began, the board of the hospital wanted me to take an extended leave because they thought the pressure of it all would greatly affect me. I appreciated their concern, but declined to take the time off. When you know who you really are, you can face any battle that come your way.

"Just imagine if I had become a politician. I may have made a good one, but I would have probably been miserable. Medicine is what gives me life. Sometimes I perform 15-hour surgeries, which can be stressful because you are dealing with matters of life or death, but I rarely feel tired. All I need is a little rest and I can swing back into action again. Knowing who you are will save you a lot of heartache. A person without the knowledge of their true identity may tend to seek applause and recognition in the wrong places. Sometimes if they are wealthy, they may flaunt their wealth in a way that makes that wealth an eyesore. Now this is not to say that anyone who is flamboyant with his or her wealth has an identity crisis. On the other hand if they are poor, they could be poseurs, always wanting to impress with the cars they drive or homes they live in, even if they are borrowing heavily to fund that lifestyle.

"A healthy self-esteem comes from knowing and accepting who you are. If you are confident in yourself, you will never feel pressured to live like the Joneses or engage in any activity society is prescribing for you. You can say no to things that are not you and you won't feel an ounce of guilt. You can reject society's expectations of you if they don't conform to what you know you were sent here on earth to do. I remember when I was in Stuttgart in Germany some years back on a secondment to Klinikum Hospital. I rode to work on a bicycle for the entire six months I lived there. Some colleagues thought a leading surgeon like me should possibly be driven to work in the latest Mercedes Benz. I understood where they came from, but I couldn't care less about their opinions of me. Men's opinions can be likened to seasons: here today and gone tomorrow.

"During this trial do you know the amount of hate mail I have received? I have received letters from people calling me a murderer and all sorts of names. Thankfully I don't open my mail anymore. My secretary handles it and gives me a heads-up every now and again on what's important. In the same vein, I have received numerous letters from people expressing love and solidarity with me. If I responded to all this, I would feel hated one day, and feel loved the next day. That is too much emotional torture. I know I am loved by my creator whether I feel like it or not. He has said to me several times that *he loves me with an everlasting love and that he will be with me even till the end of the age.*

"Abdul, to be all you are meant to be, you must get your identity right—otherwise you will spend your years on this earth seeking validation from others. If you seek others to validate you or your assignment, you will never live with conviction. If you told friends who had no knowledge in running a chemical plant that you wanted to set one up, they might give you all the reasons why such a business won't work. But in truth, you may be well suited for that business and ready to build it. Most often, revolutionaries in business, the arts, science or politics went against the herd when they came up with an invention or made history with a breakthrough.

"Without conviction, you will waiver when you encounter opposition and you may abandon your dreams. Abdul, my identity does not come from what I have, or from my reputation. If it did, what would happen to me if a junior colleague had overtaken me as the world's leading neurosurgeon? What would happen to me if I lost my car or house? If those were the source of my identity, I may not have survived this lawsuit.

"It's unfortunate, but most people have this all wrong. Because they don't know who they are, they clamor to be seen in expensive clothes or drive certain car brands to feel part of the elite clique. Why do you think gangs exist? If we all knew who we really are, there would be no gangs."

After this interesting chat, we headed off for The Royal College of Surgeons. The talk was stimulating. Even though Alex's talk was peppered with neurosurgical jargons, I learnt a myriad of things.

For me, being there meant volumes. The quality of the participants was incredible. There were surgeons and consultants from Europe, Africa and the Middle East. Alex spoke on the subject of *"Neurosurgery in the 21st Century."* After the talk, he stayed on for a little while to speak to some colleagues. During this time, I hobnobbed with some influential surgeons. I spoke extensively to one of the leading neurosurgeons in the Middle East, Dr. Khalid from Doha in Qatar. During our conversation, all the science I studied years ago came flooding back to me.

Then Alex and I were together again.

"Abdul, let's move on quickly to Great Ormond Children's Hospital. And do bear with me; I will be silent now until the lecture is over. For me, silence before an important event is essential to gather my thoughts and review what I have studied. It's also a time I stay open to receive fresh insight."

By 3pm, the lecture was over and I was starving and looking forward to eating something delicious.

Alex said, "Abdul, I will take you to one of my favourite restaurants in town. It's a Singaporean restaurant in Mayfair. Now that my duties for the day have been discharged, I can go back to sharing with you. The second principle I will like to share with you is humility. I am sure you sometimes wonder how I became this person."

"Alex, how do you seem to know most often what I am thinking?"

"Well, I guess you can say I am experienced. I realized that to be of service to humanity, I needed to study psychology so I could better understand human behavior. I read books by Abraham

Maslow, who is considered the father of modern psychology, and also books by Norman Vincent Peale. What I did was set a target of reading one psychology book a month. I also attended some of the best psychology courses. As I am in the medical field, finding such courses was effortless. Humility however came after encountering some challenging situations over the years. When I began my career 35 years ago, I thought I knew it all. I was proud and full of myself. Thanks to the challenges I've faced, I am a better person now.

"Pain is a great teacher of humility so, don't run away from pain. Pain can do you more good than harm if you extract the lessons it teaches you. The story of Matsushita Konosuke, which I will now share with you should encourage you a great deal."

CHAPTER TWO

The Value of Pain

"Out of suffering have emerged the strongest souls; the most massive characters are seared with scars."

— Khalil Gibran

Konosuke Matsushita, founder of Panasonic Electronics, is a clear example of what one can achieve in the midst of adversity. In his book *Matsushita Leadership: Lessons from the 20th Century's Most Remarkable Entrepreneur,* John P. Kotter mentioned that "Making the decision to write a biography about an interesting business leader, Matsushita certainly fitted the bill, as his life provided fascinating clues as to the roots of great leadership and to the process by which adaptive organizations are developed. But Konosuke Matsushita's saga, I found, is far more than a business story. It is about overcoming enormous adversity and drawing strength from trauma."

Konosuke Matsushita was born on 27th November 1894 in the farming village of Wasamura in the Wakayama prefecture in the Kansai region of Japan. Although Wasamura was a tiny village with only sixty houses, the Matsushita name was respected because the family had lived in that village for at least three or four generations. Masakusu, Konosuke's dad, was also elected to the village assembly. As the last child of eight, Konosuke lived a peaceful and carefree life.

He fished, played tag and just had fun.

However in 1899, the family's economic fortune collapsed and money become tight, so the ten-person household was forced to move to a two- or three-bedroom house in a back alley in Honmachi, Wakayama. Honmachi was a big town with a population of about 64,000 inhabitants. Because of their financial crisis, food was hard to come by. As if there weren't enough problems, tragedy then struck. In October 1900, Hachiro, the fourth child who was eighteen years old, caught an infectious disease and died. The loss was painful to the family; however, only six months after in April 1901, Fusae, the third child, also died tragically. Death came knocking at the door of the Matsushita's again in August 1901. This time, it was the second-born Isaburo. He was only 24 years old. So within one year, the family had lost three children. The loss of the three children and the insurmountable poverty was agonizing. In 1901, the young Konosuke began school, but due to his family's abject poverty, he was sent to school in an old uniform made partially of silk. This unorthodox uniform differentiated him from his friends—he just didn't fit in. In 1903, Masakusu moved to Osaka to find work. He found a clerical job in a school for children with disabilities. His income, though meager, brought some stability to his family. However, things were to change for the young Konosuke, who was now the only son.

While in Osaka, Masakusu learnt that a charcoal room-heater dealer was searching for an apprentice so he sent for Konosuke immediately, telling his mother Tokue that as Konosuke was already in his fourth year of primary school and would soon be graduating, this was an opportunity that couldn't be missed. So in November 1904 nine-year-old Konosuke was sent to Osaka to work and live with his employer. The sixteen-hour workday was grueling for a nine-year-old. His work consisted of babysitting his master's children, running errands, and cleaning the home and shop. As time went on, he was given more responsibility in the hibachi store.

After only three month's work, the owner decided to close the retail section of the store, making Konosuke redundant and uprooting him yet again. His father found him a job in a bicycle shop run by Otokichi Godai. Konosuke spent six years working in this bicycle shop. The work was laborious and taxing. However, he learnt various business lessons—cost management, customer service, and merchandising—which served him well when he ventured out on his own. But tragedy struck the family again in 1906. In April, Hana, the sixth-born died suddenly, and then tragedies built on each other: Only one month later, Chiyo, the fifth-born also died. In September of that same year, Masakusu, their father, who was only 51 years old, fell ill and died.

So now out of a family of 10, only 4 were alive: their mother Tokue, Iwa, Ai, and Konosuke. Despite the pain, Konosuke soldiered on. In 1909, at the age of 15, Konosuke ended his apprenticeship to scout for other opportunities. His dream was to work for the Osaka Electric Light Company. This dream was fulfilled in 1910 when a vacancy in the interior wiring section of the Saiwaicho office became available. His job was to offer simple wiring services in homes and shops. Because of his willingness to learn and his work ethic, within three months he was transferred to a newly opened branch and promoted to installation technician. This job proved to be intellectually stimulating because the electricity industry was new and the tasks were diverse. No two days were the same.

Osaka was a bustling port city with a population of over 900,000. Thanks to his job, he met scores of people. In 1912, Konosuke and fourteen other colleagues were sent to work on a project that required them to live on the site. In addition to this assignment, the many other big projects he worked on ranged from the Tsutenkaku Tower (a tower similar to the Eiffel Tower) to wiring mansions of successful business owners. These experiences proved pivotal in shaping his business philosophy. By the age of twenty, Konosuke was handling complex projects with dozens of employees under his supervision. Through his assignments, he begun meeting the aristocrats of Osaka and was exposed to their affluent lifestyles.

Just as his life had stabilized and he was making progress, tragedy struck again. In 1913, his beloved mother Tokue died. She was only fifty-seven years old. After the death of his mother, Konosuke married Mumeno, a nineteen-year-old domestic servant from Awaji Island. Mumeno was a strong-minded and competitive woman who did a lot to fan the flames of her ambitious husband. Two years into their married life, Konosuke was promoted to the level of inspector. At 22 years old, he was one of the youngest persons in the company to occupy this position, but it was a position he enjoyed for only six months. He found out the position involved only 4 hours of serious work a day. He was idle and felt empty. He invested the free time available to him after his 4-hour day job into designing a light socket that he felt was superior to the one the company sold. He presented this superior model to his boss, who was unimpressed and refused to show it to anyone else in the company.

With a growing sense of restlessness and the passion to manufacture his own sockets, Konosuke left Osaka Electric Light Company.

Even though only 22 years old, Konosuke started his own business with four employees: his wife, two former co-workers and the younger brother of his wife. The Matsushita factory was established inside his two-bedroom house, using a tiny 13-square-meter space. Apart from Konosuke, all the others were amateurs in the field. Money was tight, so they had no choice but to work seven days a week. Since the sockets they spent months building didn't sell and things were tough, two of the staff left leaving Konosuke, his wife and brother-in-law. Though they were dispirited and had to pawn clothing and personal items to make ends meet, they didn't give up. With a stroke of fortune, a wholesaler placed an order of one thousand insulation plates, asking them to be delivered within a month. Because they worked 18-hour days, 7 days a week, they delivered and made a profit of 80 yen.

This breakthrough was what they needed. Firstly it reminded Konosuke that he wasn't on a wild goose chase and it also put money in their pockets, money they desperately needed to stay afloat. In January 1918, they received an order for two thousand insulation plates from the same wholesaler. After this second order, word went around that the firm could deliver speedily, with products 30 percent cheaper than the competition. In March, they moved to a bigger factory and began hiring staff.

By October of 1918, Konosuke had 20 staff and four products. Even though business was picking up, his health was failing. Despite his weakness and high blood pressure, his enthusiasm and self-belief never waned. He worked harder and harder with each passing day. In 1919 in the midst of his growing business and ill health, tragedy struck again. This time, it was his twenty-eight-year-old sister Ai, the seventh-born who died. Two years later, Iwa, the first-born also died. She was forty-seven years old. So by the age of 27, Konosuke had lost nine members of his immediate family. Even though his personal life was in turmoil, Matsushita Electric was expanding rapidly, with a new ultra-modern factory built in 1922. The same year, they recognized the growing bicycle market and created a new product line, a bicycle lamp. This lamp was a success: by September 1924, the company was churning out 10,000 units a month. By 1926, the company began manufacturing radio parts, an iron, and dry-cell batteries.

By the end of 1928 Matsushita Electric had over three hundred employees. Mumeno bore two children, Sachiko, a girl in 1920 and Koichi, a boy in 1926. Konosuke was happy to have a son. Concerning his birth, he said, "I felt myself to be the most fortunate of men." In January 1927 when returning from a business trip in Tokyo, Konosuke received a telegram saying that Koichi was ill. On arrival in Osaka, he went straight to see Koichi, but things were not looking good—Koichi was in a coma. The coma lasted for two weeks and then tragedy struck yet again: Koichi died.

Matsushita Electric continued innovating, cutting costs, providing superior customer service, and placing value on its employees. These strategies enhanced substantial growth, despite the great depression of 1929. By 1930, 200,000 bicycle lamps and one million dry-cell batteries were produced; also in that same year, radio sets were among the products rolled out. By 1942 Matsushita Electric owned a 30-percent market share of Japan's radio market, producing 30,000 units a month and employing over 6,500 staff. Konosuke told employees at a gathering in 1932 that the mission of Matsushita Electric was to "… overcome poverty, to relieve society as a whole from misery and bring it wealth."

As success came, Konosuke saw the danger in becoming arrogant, a character (and company) trait he sought to dispel. He developed a pamphlet that spelt out the company's mission and goals. Among other things he said, "I have gradually come to believe that we must cooperate with each other in order to attain mutual prosperity and create lives filled with welfare. I realize, however that enlarging the scale of a business easily invites looseness in management, and readily breeds arrogance among personnel. We must take the utmost care to stop this from happening."

With World War II looming, Matsushita Electric ventured into shipbuilding in April 1943. This was a new venture, as Konosuke recounted, "It was not as if we already had shipbuilding facilities at our disposal. We did not have land, the workers, the technology, or the capital required for such a venture. We had been asked to perform a feat of magic, to make wooden ships out of thin air." In December, after working long days and hours and cutting out holidays, the first ship was built. After the bombings of Hiroshima and Nagasaki and the surrender of Japan, the country was plunged into an economic depression. The war devastated the Japanese economy and cost the lives of millions. One estimate places the number of buildings destroyed at 2,252,0000.

Even more troubles were ahead for Matsushita Electric, as 39 factories out of the 70 were confiscated by other nations, production ceased, and Konosuke was forced out of his own company. By April 1947, staff was reduced from 27,000 to 7,926. It was an extremely difficult time for Konosuke. He suffered from panic attacks, insomnia, and even resorted to drinking. But 1950 was a regeneration point in Matsushita Electric because Konosuke was back at the helm of its affairs. He re-instituted all the principles that built the company in the first place and created new and better ways of operation. On July 17th, at a management meeting he gave them a talk that communicated his deepest wishes for the company and galvanized everyone. "Over the five years since the end of the war, Matsushita Electric has faced one problem after another. But even when confronted with adversity, we threw ourselves into the tasks that had to be done and worked as hard as we could. We have at long last reached the point where we see light at the end of the tunnel. Now we have a whole new mission to fulfill as a company, and when I think of Japan's reconstruction, I feel a tremendous sense of hope that inspires my work." Matsushita Electric, manufacturers of Panasonic products grew and became one of the largest electronic corporations in the world. Their range of products include TVs, mobile phones, cameras, computers, aircraft in flight entertainment systems and many others. In January 2008, Matsushita Electric changed its name to Panasonic Corporation to harmonize with its Panasonic brand.

"Abdul, the war years taught Konosuke many lessons, one of them being that he used difficult experiences to learn and grow. Looking at the personal tragedy Matsushita went through, you can see where his passion and energy came from. They came from pain and how he harnessed that pain. Because of its energizing quality, pain when used positively can be a catalyst to greatness. Some consequences of pain are life after a birth, or the metaphoric birth of new dreams, joy, fulfillment, pleasure. Look at what happens when a tree is pruned or sheds its leaves naturally. It regains more leaves, which are lush and plentiful, more than it previously had. Pain can be used as fuel to attain greatness. Who would have thought that a person who navigated through a sea of personal tragedies could go on and build one of the world's largest electronic corporations.

"So! Next time you are going through some degree of pain, remember that it is your catalyst to your next level. Move through the pain, and rise to new heights."

"Alex I am dumbfounded by Matsushita's story. What he faced is simply inconceivable. How on earth can a person triumph in such adversity? Matsushita's story is one I should read every quarter. Reading it will remind me to perpetually put things in perspective. Thank you very much for sharing this."

"It is always a pleasure. My calm and confident reaction to this trial is as a result of the trials I have also faced in the past. You know, God always sends trials to toughen and prepare us for the future. Just look at the situations David the shepherd boy faced on his way to becoming King of Israel. Once when he was tending his father's sheep in the bush, the sheep were attacked by a lion and a bear. However he killed them all with his bare hands. Just imagine a lion attacking one of your sheep out of the ninety-nine you have. Wouldn't you run away leaving the lion to feast on 'just one' sheep? But not David. He fought and defeated the lion.

"Some years after those events he was faced with a similar situation. This time around it was a nine-foot giant called Goliath. Goliath openly boasted about his strength and prowess. His sword, spear, and amour alone weighed thousands of pounds. David, who was only five-feet tall, went into this battle with a sling and a stone. He believed that the war would be fought and won supernaturally. And just as David predicted, he defeated Goliath and killed him with his own sword. David had the courage to fight Goliath because of the trials he overcame while tending his father's sheep.

"Just like I recounted to you earlier, I have overcome many trials to get here. In our early years of marriage, Jean and I were looking to adopt a baby from Cambodia. After searching far and wide, we found a beautiful girl called Angel. Angel was all and more that we imagined. She was happy and had one of the most electrifying smiles I had ever seen. Angel was malnourished, so she was rather tiny. I remember a few friends wondering how old she was. When I said she was two years old they were surprised because in actual fact she looked more like a one-year-old. At the time, I was working at the Royal Phnom Penh Hospital in Cambodia. We went through the adoption process for nearly a year. When she joined us at home we were on cloud nine, very, very happy. We were thankful to have been given the opportunity to be part of building Angel's life.

"After one month of having Angel, her parents came back asking that we return her. They said they didn't want to go ahead with the adoption any longer. We were devastated. How could this happen to us? Initially, we wanted to contest the matter in court; however, upon careful consideration, we decided not to. Angel's birth parents promised to pay some of the monies back but we told them to keep it. It was one of the most traumatic times in our lives. After carefully praying about the situation, we let go knowing that *All things will work together for our good because we love the Lord and are called according to his purpose.'*

"After God brought us through that situation, we knew without a shadow of doubt that he would bring us through any trials that we will face. And like I have told you time and time again that once you live on planet earth, you are bound to face tests. My advice to you is to face them head on - never run away from tough situations because when you do you will not be promoted to the next level.

"Some years ago, I was tipped to become the Chairman of the Council of the British Medical Association. This is a position I really wanted, because I thought I was well suited for the job. I was experienced and I worked extremely hard. In my mind, the position was mine because compared to the other five candidates, I was more experienced and had better credentials. On the day of the selection, I wasn't chosen. The panel chose someone who was about 15 years my junior. This guy, who was 40 years old, was at one point my student. I taught him in medical school. So you can imagine how I felt. I was crushed. The newspapers and some medical journals even expressed surprise about the choice of candidate.

"For days I felt humiliated. I walked with my head bowed. However in retrospect, I can tell you that public shame and humiliation brought me a great deal of humility, and I am thankful for it. Don't run away from public humiliation, Abdul. You may be hurt, broken, laughed at, and scorned, but humility is not birthed any other way. Unfortunately, when most people face public humiliation, the first thing they do is fight or take flight. Like Adam in the Garden of Eden, they hide. Whenever you run away from a situation like that, you won't learn the lessons; you won't learn humility. This leads me to another important point in your quest for success: Forgiveness.

"In order to live life with joy, and peace, you must forgive anyone who may have offended you. Lewis B. Smedes hit the nail on the head when he said, *'To forgive is to set the prisoner free and discover that the prisoner was you.'* You may be thinking, forgive my father or mother who abused me? Forgive my husband or wife who ran off with another person? Forgive that business partner who stole from me?

"One thing you must remember is our imperfection as humans. If you acknowledge that you have also hurt others in the past you will not hesitate to forgive anyone who offends you. Now, don't confuse forgiveness with reconciliation. They are two different things. In some cases the offender may even be dead, making reconciliation impossible.

"I will share a personal story you can relate to. Years ago, someone I called a friend tried forging my signature on a very important document in the hospital. Unbeknown to me, this person hated me and wanted me removed from my position as head of department. Abdul, it was just fortune that saved me—I really would have been in deep trouble. When I was queried, I said I had no knowledge of signing it and thankfully because of my credibility, a forensic test I requested was granted. After the forensic test, the truth emerged that it wasn't my signature and the search to find the culprit began. I suspected this person but I tried not to dwell on it, since I didn't have any evidence.

"After a thorough investigation, the culprit was arrested and prosecuted. Initially I was aggrieved, and a part of me was seeking revenge, but I knew that I needed to forgive him in order to experience joy on a daily basis. Eventually, I forgave him and I even went a step further by giving him some money when he needed to pay his daughter's school fees. He was severely penalized for his offence. Truthfully I could have been sent to jail, because the document he signed authorized our department to purchase equipment that cost 500,000 Euros, equipment we actually didn't need. All they had to say for me to be jailed was that I had connived with the supplier to defraud the hospital.

"If you come to understand that people who are hurt, hurt other people in turn, you will be quick to forgive. When you also understand that people see things differently from each other, and this difference may cause offence between you and others, you will forgive. Also you must remember that a person will act based on what they know. So if as a child your mother physically abused you, you have to realize that she may not have known any better. She may have been saddled with issues making her incapable of showing you affection or correcting you using other methods.

"That is why you should never hold a grudge against your parents. If you are considerate of them you will forgive them. How many parents today read books on how to become a better parent? In the last two years Abdul, have you read any books to learn how to be an effective parent? Please be honest with me."

"No, I haven't Alex," I replied.

"So how can you say that all the ways you have related to your children have been the right ways? You may have made a lot of mistakes. Even your daily absence and unavailability to help them with their homework may make them resent you in the future. Would you say you were happy to be away from home?"

I said, "No I wasn't happy, but demands on my finances and the tension at home are the cause of my absence."

Alex asked, "But did you know that your physical presence at home gives them a stable foundation?"

"No, I didn't know."

"Well there you go—now you understand what I mean. You also have to accept the fact that humans make mistakes, so you must forgive. In a groundbreaking forgiveness research project, by Stanford University and detailed in his book *Forgive for Good*, Dr. Fred Luskin cites many benefits of forgiveness. He actually calls this the science of forgiveness. This is what Fred Luskin had to say. 'Preliminary studies from research in allied fields such as psychology, medicine and religion show that more positive emotions such as gratitude, faith and care have a positive impact on cardiovascular functioning. People who evidence higher degrees of blame suffer more from a variety of illnesses. Medical and psychological studies have shown for years that anger and hostility are harmful to cardiovascular health.'

"All this research points to the fact that the benefits of forgiveness are innumerable. What is remarkable about Dr. Luskin's forgiveness training projects is that in one of such projects he conducted in Northern Ireland, he brought together both Catholic and Protestant women who had lost a son to murder. Before the project, their feelings of hurt on a scale of 1–10 registered an 8.5. By the end of the project and six months after undertaking the training, their hurt was below 4. These women reported a significant increase in being optimistic and hopeful about their lives and future. Their depression levels had also been reduced significantly.

Just listen to this passage from the Message translation of the bible about forgiveness, you will be aghast: "*You are familiar with the old written law, Love your friend, and its unwritten companion, hate your enemy. I am challenging that. I'm telling you to love your enemies. Let them bring out the best in you, not the worst. When someone gives you a hard time, respond with the energies of prayer, for then you are working out of your true selves, your God-created selves. This is what God does. He gives his best—the sun to warm and the rain to nourish—to everyone, regardless: the good and bad, the nice and nasty. If all you do is love the lovable, do you expect a bonus? Anyone can do that. If you simply say hello to those who greet you, do you expect a medal? Any run-of-the-mill sinner does that. In a word, what I'm saying is, grow up. You're kingdom subjects. Now live like it. Live out your God-created identity. Live generously and graciously towards others, the way God lives toward you."*

"The subject of forgiveness is encyclopedic, so I suggest you spend a few good months studying about it. Also, apply what you learn. When you apply what you learn, you will become a bona fide student of the subject."

After settling the bill at the restaurant, Alex thanked the waitress and also the head chef before leaving.

"Abdul, I make it a point to say thank you to the chef whenever I come here. I find thanking the chef gratifying because diners by and large do not thank the chef; the chef is hidden. If the chef is busy, what I do is write him or her a note. I know this will enliven their day. I particularly go out of my way to thank those whose jobs are hidden. On every occasion I fly on an airplane, I write letters of appreciation for the pilots. I also pray for them because they do a terrific job flying us safely to our destinations and to our families. Never miss an opportunity to thank anyone who serves you."

I replied, "Alex, I am indebted to you for the sacrifices you have made for me. Leaving you is always a battle. I just want to cry."

"Go ahead Abdul, cry if you want to. Shedding tears of joy or appreciation is not a sign of weakness. Truly, it is a sign of strength. In doing so, you are being human, you are being authentic. Thank you very much for delighting in all that I share. Sharing what I have learnt with others gives me life. I wholeheartedly enjoy teaching. I will take the tube to Waterloo station so you can go and serve more clients."

I drove off with mixed emotions: elation, anguish, and gratitude. I was thankful to be alive and to have been given the opportunity to learn all these life-changing lessons. Now, to think I could have gone through life without learning any of these lessons made me even more grateful.

When I got home, I indulged in the bath ritual and drank one full glass of water. I felt energized. After teaching the children, I settled down to read the second book Alex gave me, *Change Your Thinking, Change Your Life* by Brian Tracy.

I woke up the next morning in high spirits. I went for a 30-minute walk through Plashet Park, not far from where I live. I couldn't believe I went walking. The weather was cold and crisp but nice. Since meeting Alex, I noticed that I had become happier. My circumstances hadn't changed, but I had stopped wallowing in misery and self-pity. Rather, I was focused on finding solutions to the challenges I was facing. My outlook on life had altered tremendously.

As a result of this joy, I started cutting back on working to my grave and began spending time with the children. My daily walks were consistent, and I read for an hour every day. Before I met Alex, I would talk to my friends after work, but after our encounter I wasn't interested in calling them anymore because the conversations we had did not add value to me; rather, they devalued me and fueled my doubts and fears. Thankfully I had books to occupy me.

At 8:50am, I was parked outside St. Thomas Hospital.

At 9:00am exactly, Alex came to the car.

I asked, "You are always on time Alex, how do you do it?"

Alex replied, "Well, Abdul, I am generally on time because I respect others. Time, they say, is money and this is a principle I live. When you place a premium on your time and the time of others, you send a signal to them that they are esteemed. If I am late, my lateness affects every other meeting of mine and of others. So I do my best to be on time. Now, I am not rigid about this—I know I could be held up for various reasons like a train cancellation, the weather, flight delays and all. However, I normally make room for these delays by adding an allowance of 30 minutes to my meeting times. If I am early, I simply spend the time listening to the dozens of audio books on my iPod so I don't waste the time. It is important to respect the time of others.

"Today, we will be going to the courts for an hour and then I will be giving lectures at the University College London, my alma mater. I want you to be part of the lecture, and this time around, I want you to ask some questions during the question-and-answer session. This means you have to pay particular attention to what I will say. Don't be afraid that your question might reveal to others that you are not in the medical field. Bear in mind that it is in being curious that we learn. And who cares if you are laughed at? As bestselling author Seth Godin once said, *'I found out that I didn't die when I was laughed at'*. You must develop the skin of the porcupine if you want to be successful. If you don't have a thick skin, you will forever be at the mercy of others' opinions, which vacillate anyway.

"Did you hear what I said earlier about the opinions of men? Let me say it again: man's opinions are like the four seasons, here today and gone tomorrow. When you have a thick skin and you make a mistake, you will acknowledge your mistake but you won't spend your precious time worrying about what the town gossips are saying about you. Listen, mistakes are a part of mastery. You will make oodles of mistakes in your quest to attain mastery. Embrace them, because the more mistakes you are making, the more you are learning and achieving mastery. Also, the tougher your skin, the less you will feel bruised. You will always learn to see things from a higher perspective. While I am on this subject of mistakes, let me add this important lesson about naysayers, gossips and critics: Have you ever seen a plaque or statue in honor of a critic or gossip? Critics and gossips have no monuments erected for them. They are forgotten immediately they leave this earth.

"Do you know the name of any of Michelangelo's critics? Critics die with their name, but the name of a distinguished person lives on and on. People who criticize you sometimes have a point. They may be trying to make you look at things more carefully, so don't dismiss the input critics can have. Some are also jealous of you. A person criticizing you out of jealousy may be doing so because they do not have the capacity to do what you are doing. When the Eiffel Tower was under construction in 1887, one critic ridiculed it as a 'high and skinny pyramid of iron ladders.'

"A critic's comments about the Royal Ontario Museum are one of my favourite examples. The Royal Ontario Museum's main entrance, designed by Daniel Libeskind, was opened in 2007. This magnificent building, made of glass and steel, is called the Crystal. This building is one I am fascinated and intrigued by. I loved this building so much that I took many pictures of it when I went to Toronto some years ago to speak in one of the leading hospitals. This is what one critic said about the museum, 'The new Royal Ontario Museum rages at the world; it's oppressive, angsty and hellish.' So there you go. What one person appreciates, another may detest.

"Abraham Lincoln was called all manner of names. He was once called a grotesque baboon, an ape, and a buffoon. He said that 'Any leader will be criticized. How you handle it will determine whether you succeed or fail.' In Lawrence G. Lovasik's words, *'Only the ignorant and narrow-minded gossip, for they speak of persons instead of things.'*

"Abdul, another lesson I would like to share with you is about conflict resolution. You must acquire the necessary knowledge and tools for resolving conflicts. Understand that as long as you are walking on the face of this earth, you are bound to have conflict with others. Now conflict in itself is not a bad thing. Conflict can be an opportunity for learning and growth, but for many people, conflict is a sign to run away, shut down, or fight back. Conflicts occur in every relationship, be it a business, a love-based relationship, a parent/child relationship, or a doctor/patient relationship. You will have conflicts with other human beings; it is natural to disagree with others.

"Let me give you a brief description of the brain. All human beings have a left brain and a right brain. The left brain is the logical and analytical side. It is the part of the brain that enjoys science, math, and languages. The right brain is the creative side. It enjoys arts and music and views things in a holistic way. So a person who tends to be analytical and wants to see facts and figures before making a decision is likely to disagree with their colleague who is creative and is sometimes up in the clouds. This difference in how we use our brains can spark some serious conflicts.

"Secondly, our upbringing, culture and worldview shape us, so a person with a different upbringing and culture from you can stir up conflict. I remember when Jean and I got married; we used to have regular quarrels about small things, like our Christmas day celebrations. Even though the quarrels were small, they could end in big arguments. In my family, Christmas was low key, no big deal. We had our cousins, aunties, uncles and friends come over.

Sometimes when the day ended, we would have hosted about 30 guests. For us the main focus was on the company.

"However in Jean's family, Christmas day dinner would have only about 10 members of the family and the focus was on the decorations, the ambiance of the room, the dinner table, the Christmas crackers, and the clothes they wore. For them it was a formal dinner where everyone dressed up. I used to be infuriated with all the work that went into these kinds of gatherings. I saw the effort as unnecessary. My opinion was that let's invite as many family members as possible, cook a variety of dishes and have drinks available—that is it. We shouldn't spend money buying design serviettes, elaborate tablecloths, unique Christmas decorations and certainly no Christmas crackers. Thank God we finally saw the light to understand that our conflicts were arising because of our different upbringing.

"Another area we would fight about was our holidays. I love traveling, but Jean doesn't enjoy travelling that much. When she travels, she enjoys visiting a familiar place or places with endless numbers of art galleries like Paris, Rome, or New York. I am the complete opposite. I don't usually visit a city twice for a holiday. I can't stand going to the same city over and over again. For me, travel is about discovering new places. Travel is about the unknown. Stability, familiarity, and comfort are the last things I seek when I am on the road. But thankfully we came to an agreement that has worked very well for us. Every year, I travel with Jean to a familiar place or a place of her choice for a week and then I am free to visit three or four new cities alone without her. On some of my travels, I go with the children and she stays at home to paint.

"Sometimes conflicts can arise due to our own insecurities and pain from our childhood. Conflicts can also arise due to unresolved issues from our past. I remember a wealthy client once commissioned Jean to paint a series of art pieces. It was quite an expensive project. She wanted Jean to produce about 20 different pieces of art. This client was moving into a 5,000sqm home and wanted the paintings ready before her housewarming party. Now Jean always delivers on time—if you think I am punctual, wait until you meet Jean—but during the months leading to this deadline, our son Paul, who suffers from Down Syndrome, was in and out of hospital. So Jean couldn't pay 100% attention to her work.

"When Jean called six weeks from the deadline explaining the situation to the client, she was livid. The client behaved in a manner that astounded us. She went into a rage and even threatened to sue us. Her behavior was simply abnormal, so we decided to investigate this. Unknown to us, Jean looked like the client's mother, who had abandoned her as a child. She was raised by her father.

"So in effect her anger was not caused by the delay in the paintings per se. The anger was caused because Jean reminded the client of her absent mother. After this revelation, our relationship with her improved. We actually settled the matter amicably, and by a miracle Jean finished the work a day before the deadline. Can you imagine not being privy to this information? We may have been in court for a very long time. Conflicts also arise whenever we pledge allegiance to a particular group and tend to think of those of those outside that group as our enemies. This is very common in religion, politics, and in sports. A person who supports Manchester United may see Chelsea supporters as enemies.

"In American politics, a person who is a Republican tends to look at Democrats as enemies. They seem to forget that the matter at hand is in choosing a candidate who will run the country smoothly. If a Democrat runs the country to the ground, all Democrats as well as all Republicans will suffer. It is unfortunate, but many tend to think that their party alone has the solution to running the country.

"I once heard a story about where wisdom can be found. Kwaku Ananse, a very wise man, was asked by God to collect all the wisdom he could find and put it in a pot. After this arduous task, Ananse decided to hide his pot of wisdom in the tallest tree, where he alone would have access to it. Ananse succeeded in lugging the pot all the way to the top of the tree in the thick forest. However, as he was strapping the pot to the tree, the pot of wisdom fell and broke and all the contained wisdom scattered to every corner in the world.

"So truthfully no human being is the custodian of all the wisdom in the world. If you understand this, you will be open-minded and be willing to listen to others' viewpoints, which will enable you to solve conflicts as they arise. In resolving conflicts there are various factors to consider, but I will touch on only a few. First, you must realize that every conflict is caused by all the people involved. As much as I would like to think that Jean is the sole cause of every conflict we have, the fact of the matter is that I am also a contributor to them. It is so easy to point fingers at the other person and exonerate ourselves.

"Secondly, you have to learn to put yourself in the other person's shoes. Grasping where the other party is coming from will help diffuse anger that may be welling up and help you find a solution. Like I said earlier, if we did not seek to understand Jean's client, we may have been in a legal battle now. After that incident, our relationship with her was strengthened and Jean has now sold about twenty more pieces of art to her. This client has introduced us to numerous friends who have all ended up buying some art pieces from Jean.

"Thirdly, you have to learn to empathize with others. Never forget that every one you meet is dealing with one issue or the other. For some it's a challenge with their health, for others it's their finances, their relationships, or business, or career. You should know that fundamentally human beings are good and have good intentions. But sometimes due to some factors they will step on a toe or two. Also, know that all human beings—whether you like them or not—are made in the image and likeness of God. Once you grasp this truth, you can empathize with others and also treat them with respect.

"Look at it this way: if you were walking down the road and met God, how would you treat him? Have this consciousness about man, and your life will be-stress free. Lastly, you have to be a forgiving person. Without forgiveness there will always be war raging within you. Thomas Fuller said it well: 'He that cannot forgive others breaks the bridge over which he must pass himself; for every man has need to be forgiven.' Learn to resolve conflicts and you will be a happy man."

"Thanks a lot Alex; I never saw it that way. I used to be the guy who would take flight at the first sign of a conflict. Going forward, I will stay and resolve them. I can now see how my attitude has affected Halima. She usually seeks to understand my viewpoint, but now I realize that I didn't even create that environment for discussion. How wrong I was."

"I have a gift for you, Abdul—it is a thorough book on conflict resolution. It's titled *Conflict in Relationships, Understand It, Overcome It: at Home, at Work, in Life*. I want you to make a promise to me that you will read this book once every year to remind yourself of the need to resolve conflicts."

"I promise you Alex, I will."

"How did you find the lecture, by the way?"

"Alex, I was bowled over. I had no idea the brain could perform such extraordinary tasks. And knowing the brain has the capacity to grow has altered my thinking completely. I will stretch it until it grows bigger and bigger. And as you said in the talk, 'Learning does to the brain what weightlifting does to the body.'

"Thanks, Abdul for asking the questions. I salute your courage. Courage is a trait most people don't develop and this is unfortunate because courage is a necessity in your quest to be successful. Without courage you will not take any compelling steps and thereby you will not make any impact. Aristotle said it perfectly when he said that, 'You will never do anything in this world without courage. It is the greatest quality of the mind next its optimal functionality.'

"Without courage I surely would not be where I am today. I already told you the threat letters I have received during this trial. Without courage my head would have been permanently bowed. I just don't focus on the letters; I always remind myself why I am here and what I have been asked to do. Does this mean I am not afraid sometimes? No, not at all. There is nothing significant I have wanted to do without feeling afraid.

"What I have learnt to do is go ahead irrespective of the fears, or as Susan Jeffers said, 'Feel the fear and do it anyway.' I want you to practice courage by taking small steps every day. Take small steps, but ones that usually make you cringe. These steps can be as small as walking an extra mile, or saying sorry to that person you hurt, or saving an extra twenty pounds a month, or buying an extra book a month. Like with muscles in your body, you will realize that with time, your courage muscle will be strong so you can start taking bigger steps. You must also look for creative ways to solve problems. Being an out-of-the-box thinker reminds me of a story I read of a guy who wanted to meet a successful entrepreneur in his city. His first challenge was tracking down such a busy man.

"Now you know that successful people guard their time, so tracking him down was no easy feat. Successful people loathe time wasters. However, once they know you mean business, by going about it the right way you are sure to get an audience with them. After several attempts to have an audience with him failed, the guy hatched a plan to send letters to this entrepreneur via DHL. He sent DHL letters every single day for two weeks until he secured the meeting. This strategy worked because it was creative and different, albeit expensive. You have to think differently to be able to secure such a meeting. If you don't become an out-of-the-box thinker, you will hardly make any progress. To be at the top of your game, you have to part with the phrase 'this is how it's always been done.'

"Whenever you encounter a challenge, take a pen and paper, sit down in a quiet place and force your mind to generate a minimum of 10 ideas. When you start using this method you may struggle initially, but you have to keep at it until it becomes easy. I have said this countless times: the more you exercise any muscle, the stronger it gets and the less energy you will use. Believe me if you practice this skill consistently for six months, you may even get to the place where will be able to generate 20 or 30 solutions for any challenge you may be facing. Achievers use this method in generating ideas for new projects or products so they are constantly innovating.

"Guess what? It's Jean's birthday today so we are having a special celebration this evening and we are inviting you and your family."

"What? Me and my family?" I asked, perplexed.

"Yes, you are very important to me, so it will be an honour for me to have you present. We are going to the movies to watch *Madea's Family Reunion* by Tyler Perry.

"We have also invited Jean's friends, some colleagues and students of mine. Now for us as a family, laughter is very important. Without laughter Jean and I would be stressed. As the saying goes, laughter is the best medicine. I wholeheartedly believe that. In the past 20 years, there has been a lot of research conducted into the benefits of laughter on our health and it has been proven that laughter can boost your immune system and even fight diseases. If your immune system is weak, you can easily catch colds and the flu. When the children were growing up, just to get them to understand the importance of laughter, I coined the phrase '15 minutes of laughter a day keeps colds and flu at bay.'

"Laughter also protects the heart by increasing the blood flow, which then shields your heart from cardiovascular problems. Laughter releases endorphins in the brain, which block pain and its sensation. So what happens is that the more you laugh, the less pain you feel. The pain can be related to your physical body; it can be psychological or emotional pain. If you laugh a lot, even if you may be going through a crisis, you won't feel it much. Laughter makes you happy. The more you laugh, the happier you become. Just look at children—most children are happy because they laugh a lot.

"Some statistics say that the average four-year-old laughs 300 times a day but on average, an adult laughs only four times a day. The mistake many adults make is that they stop laughing often. Most adults want to reserve laughter for a special occasion like a promotion at work, or a party. If you laugh every day, you will be happy every day. If you wait for a special event to happen before you laugh, you may end up waiting for months, and this is detrimental to your health.

"Basically I laugh at every opportunity I get. Sometimes I laugh at myself—I laugh at my crazy and not-so-perfect ways. However, once every three months or so, Jean and I attend comedy shows from comedians around the world. When you become a person who laughs, in effect a happy person, you won't lack company, because people want to be around a happy person. Also, a person who laughs a lot is rarely an angry person, because laughter diffuses negative emotions and releases positive emotions like joy and gratitude. Since laughter is contagious, the more you laugh, the more you want to laugh.

"Also, engage in fun activities like singing contests at home with the kids. Play hide and seek with them. Have fun Abdul, don't take yourself too seriously. Charlie Chaplin said 'A day without laughter is a day wasted.' So don't waste any day. In magazines, look out for riddles and articles that will make you laugh. I remember so well always looking forward to reading my parents' copy of Reader's Digest. My favourite sections were *'All in a Day's Work'* and *'Laughter Is the Best Medicine.'* Buy books with funny stories, quotes and jokes. You can actually dedicate one night a week for family joke times. This is a time to share your jokes. When you institute this ritual, you will be amazed how everyone will want to find a joke and share. Laughing will also bond you as a family. "

CHAPTER THREE

The Power of Learning

"Live as if you were to die tomorrow. Learn as if you were to live forever"

— Mahatma Gandhi

The next day, Alex and I met. "Good morning Abdul, how did you find the comedy movie yesterday? I absolutely loved it."

"You know what, Alex? I woke up laughing so much today. I just kept on replaying the scenes, Halima has been laughing too. I can honestly say that for the first time in a very long while we were happy to be in each other's company. I am amazed at what laughter can do. Halima and I have agreed to institute the weekly joke night every Friday. Thank you very much Alex for believing in me and for investing your precious time in me. I am eternally grateful."

"It is my pleasure Abdul. Your success story has just begun and I am thrilled to be part of it. I actually have another book for you. It's by Robin Sharma and it's titled *The Monk Who Sold His Ferrari.*

"Today I want to share with you the story of a famous Englishman. His story reinforces the fact that greatness resides in each and every one of us. One's willingness to learn and grow is more important than where and how one is born.

Isaac Newton was born in a farmhouse in rural Lancashire in England in 1643. His parents were farmers. At 10 he was sent off to school eight miles from home so he lodged with William Clarke, a pharmacist or medical professional. At that young age he was taught Latin, theology, Greek, Hebrew and practical arithmetic. When Isaac was 16, his mother asked him to leave school to come and tend their sheep. He was a farmer for nearly two years, but Henry Stokes his former head teacher told his mother to allow Isaac to come back to school since he was a bright and enterprising young man. When he completed Kings School, on the recommendation of his uncle, the Rev. William Ayscough, Isaac gained admission at the University of Cambridge in 1661. Because he couldn't pay his fees, he performed valet duties for three years in exchange for his education until he was awarded a scholarship in 1664.

Isaac was obsessed with education; he felt he was doing God's service by learning. He feasted on the works of Aristotle, the French philosopher and mathematician René Descartes, the German mathematician Johannes Kepler, as well as the Italian astronomer Galileo Galilei. His love for mathematics was unparalleled, so he bought a vast number of books on the subject. He completed Cambridge with a BA, but due to the bubonic plague of 1665, which killed over 100,000 people, all institutions were closed down so Isaac was home for two years. During those two years, Newton taught himself various aspects of mathematics and unknowingly became the world's paramount mathematician.

Newton returned to Cambridge in 1667 to pursue a master's degree. His professor in mathematics, Isaac Burrow, was impressed with his knowledge and he became Burrow's protégé. Burrow introduced him to other giants in the field. Burrow, who felt he was more of a theologian rather than a mathematician, resigned from his post as a Professor of Math, yielding it to Newton at the young age of 27. Newton wrote several scientific papers published by the Royal Society of London, a distinguished scientific organization dedicated to promoting science. At 29, Newton invented the first "practical" telescope and also propounded the theory of colour. He lectured on optics at Trinity College in Cambridge. In his thirties, his hair was already grey. He stayed in his room for days on end: not eating, just learning and working by candlelight.

During these years too, Newton turned to Christian theology with the same fervour with which he studied mathematics. At 44, Newton published his first book *Philosophae Naturalis Principia Mathematica.* In that book he announced his famous Law of Motion. His book was a rare find in stores: the 1,000 copies he printed were all bought by noble institutions. At 45 he started to be noticed by scientists all over the world. He then became a member of Parliament for Cambridge University. At 53 Newton left Cambridge for the Royal Mint, the organization which manufactures coins in the United Kingdom. He was made head of the mint at 56 and was at the helm for nearly 30 years. One of his innovations as the head of the mint was moving the fiscal standard of the pound from silver to gold. At 60, Newton was made the president of The Royal Society, a learned society dedicated to improving natural knowledge. He was also knighted by Queen Anne at 62.

As president of The Royal Society, he helped the organization to flourish and it became the light of all scientific research and experimentation in the whole of Europe. Even though he was a very successful man, he was modest in describing his achievements. In a letter he wrote to Robert Hooke in 1676, he said, 'If I have seen further it is by standing on the shoulders of giants.' Newton lived a full life, dying at the ripe age of 84. At his death, he owned amongst many things a vast library with nearly 2,000 books and many unpublished manuscripts. He was given a state funeral that was attended by the high and mighty in society from around the world, and he was buried in Westminster Abbey. Newton was never married and was believed to have died a virgin.

"This is Newton's story in summary. Now who would have thought that a boy who started out tending sheep would grow up to become one of the most eminent scientists in the world?

"Alex, do you know that though I am interested in science I never knew the full story of Sir Isaac Newton?"

"Well, I am not surprised Abdul. The truth of the matter is that if you don't take the time to learn and research you wouldn't know many things."

"You are right Alex. I will make learning a priority from today. One thing I feel tugging on my heart is the desire to go into politics. After I gain my law degree and I establish a law firm, I will pursue politics."

"Really, Abdul—is that what you want?"

"Yes Alex, I do."

"Ok, you know what? Let's have a conversation about this tomorrow as I have to dash off for a meeting now. Let's meet tomorrow at the usual time."

CHAPTER FOUR

Wake Up Sleeping Giant

"If a country is to be corruption free and become a nation of beautiful minds, I strongly feel there are three key societal members who can make a difference. They are the father, the mother and the teacher."

— A.P. J. Abdul Kalam, 11th President of India

"Abdul, you mentioned yesterday that you had a desire to get into politics after your law degree. Why do you want to get into politics?"

"Alex, I hate oppression in all forms—physical, political and socio-economic oppression breaks my heart. I take that measure from Thomas Jefferson, one of the founding fathers of the United States of America who rightly proclaimed in the Declaration of Independence that 'We hold these truths to be self-evident that all men are created equal; that they are endowed by their Creator with certain unalienable Rights; that among these are Life, Liberty and the pursuit of Happiness.' I believe in this statement wholeheartedly."

"Do you believe getting into politics will enable you to liberate people from the forms of injustice you detest?"

"Yes Alex, I believe that."

"So which party will you join? Labour, Conservative, Liberal Deomocrats or the Green Party?"

"I will join none of these. I will get into politics in Ghana, not in the UK. I believe that I am needed much more in Ghana. As a teenager, I was involved in debates and was always campaigning against one form of injustice or the other, both in school and in my neighbourhood. I was even nicknamed by some of my peers 'Presido,' meaning President. Then, I never envisaged my life taking this route. Of course I am to blame for the poor choices I made. But yes, I thought by this age, I would have been closer to the top. I feel I am closer to the bottom than the top."

"Abdul, I have no doubt that all you have been through will prepare you for the future. At times we tend to think that some phases of our lives are unrelated to the purpose we were created for - trust me, all of this will come together in the future to make you that change agent you were created to be. And also, you are not old at all. At 33 years old, your life can still turn out satisfactorily. We are not all early starters. While people like Mozart and Dr. Martin Luther King made their marks at a young age, there are numerous people who made history and had tremendous impact at an old age.

"The octogenarian and billionaire Peter G. Peterson, founder of the private equity firm Blackstone Group is a classic example. When he was 50 years old, nothing showed he would attain such wealth and influence in the future, for example, by funding the Peter G. Peterson Foundation in 2006 with a billion dollars. Peter started out in business, moved into politics as the United States Secretary of Commerce during the Nixon administration, then became the CEO of Lehman Brothers for 10 years. After leaving

Lehman at 59 years old, he founded Blackstone Group with Steve Schwarzman. They built the company one brick at a time under very challenging times and in Peter's own words 'It was the first two years of hell, begging, and wet shoes.' When the company went public in 2007, Peter became a billionaire—at 80 years old.

"Now back to your political ambitions. So tell me Abdul, do you just want to serve in government or do you want to be the top man?"

"I want to be the president of Ghana."

"Wow, I admire your courage. Your face lit up when you made that statement. Travelling around the world has opened my eyes to the reasons some countries are and will forever be ahead of others. Being in Scandinavia and observing how Scandinavians live bears witness to this fact. Here are some observations I have made: Scandinavians generally use the resources they have. So once snow abounds in their countries they sell snow travel or snow sports to the world. Norway is a classic example. My second observation is that Scandinavians live in sync with nature. Their homes and lives always reflect their environment.

"Actually, allow me to focus on Denmark. I have been to the Danish capital twice, which is quite unusual for me. I don't usually visit a city or country twice unless it has truly touched me. Its capital, Copenhagen, is a bicycle lover's paradise—as a cyclist I could envisage myself living there. There are bicycles everywhere. Do you know that Copenhagen has 390km of designated bicycle lanes? That is the same distance from Accra to Sunyani in Ghana, or from London to Brussels. Cycling is so ingrained in the Danish culture that everyone cycles. Bankers, lawyers, students, teachers, politicians and even toddlers as young as two years old cycle alongside their parents. One statistic I saw stated that over 60% of Parliamentarians rode a bicycle to the Danish Parliament. Can you dare to imagine the MP for your area cycling to work? What about your entire cabinet ministers with you as President all cycling to work?

"The Danes love to read. Abdul, the reading culture in Denmark is unprecedented. My visit to the National Library of Denmark (nicknamed 'The Black Diamond') further proved this. The name Black Diamond came about because of the black marble tiles, which were brought in all the way from Zimbabwe, for its exterior. This magnificent building houses over 34 million items and has 438 full-time staff. Abdul, when you become the President of Ghana, will you make learning a priority? Will you focus on policies which will aid citizens to transform their minds? Or will you be interested in nonproductive interventions like offering free loaves of bread to the citizenry or buying four-wheel drives for your cabinet ministers to ply on the deplorable roads which is a cosmetic solution. Why not fix the roads and make them safe, so that a person like me can run or to cycle to work?"

"Alex, with all that you are teaching me and what I am learning, how in God's name could I repeat the mistakes some of our leaders have made? I know you have been sent into my life for a reason. I promise, I won't disappoint you."

"I haven't actually finished narrating the story about the famous Black Diamond."

"Carry on Alex, I am all ears."

"The interior is made of glass and holds several reading rooms, both old and new. I was told that usually by 10am most of the reading rooms would be full of readers researching or learning. The Black Diamond is such a popular building that tourists visit the library for guided tours. One would think that a building as impressive as this would charge a fee for entry or usage. Visiting the library is free of charge.

"After visiting one of the main reading rooms, I was humbled by what I saw. When I came out after spending hours in this impressive library I asked myself why some nations lead and others don't. And the answer that came to me was that 'Nations lead because they learn.' A learning nation will become a leading nation. Robin Sharma hits the nail on the head when he said 'Victims love entertainment, leaders love education.'"

"Alex, I know I will have a lot of work to do when I become President, but I know God will help me make a difference."

"I know you will make a difference, Abdul.

"Denmark also has various means of transport so there isn't congestion on the roads. People walk, cycle, use cars, trains, and boats to get to work. Their transport system is one of the best in the world. According to many reports, Denmark is one of the most entrepreneurial countries in the world. Abdul, if you were a looking to start a business in Denmark, there are only four straightforward procedures you need in order to set up. Denmark exports various goods and services and obviously exports more than it imports. Its industries include manufacturing, pharmaceutical, shipbuilding, food processing, machinery, and a host of others. Where do you think Legos are made? Denmark.

"Another advantage Denmark has is that its educational policies give equal expression to science and arts. So both left-brainers and right-brainers are engaged, no group is left out. The world needs left-brainers, who are usually things like scientists, engineers, and actuaries. Right-brainers like artists, graphic designers, music composers, writers, and creatives are equally needed. Can you imagine a world without music? What about art?

"Abdul, I have personally been to the Copenhagen Opera House in the Danish capital and I can boldly say it is one of the most impressive modern buildings I have seen, and probably most impressive in the world. Do you know how much it cost to build? Its costs were over $500 million. You must see a performance here in your lifetime.

"The last and critical point is that Denmark ranks very low on corruption."

"Alex, I know transforming Ghana to become a Denmark in the future will be a tall order. But I am up for the task."

"Abdul, I will even suggest that after your law degree, you should look for a six-month stint in a Danish firm. It doesn't necessarily have to be a law firm. Working in a different area other than law for six months will expand your horizon. You will learn a lot, which will be useful in the future. And please, please, while in Denmark, make it a point to visit Norway, Sweden, Finland and Iceland.

"Abdul, have you been to Hong Kong yet?"

"Oh Alex, what a question! How could I have been to Hong Kong when I didn't see the value of travelling until I met you? I haven't even been to France, which is right next door to the UK. Unfortunately, my life used to consist of working hard and spending time with people going nowhere."

"Well then, Hong Kong is also a country you should visit and study. In 1940 Hong Kong was a small colony of the British Empire with a population of 1.6 million inhabitants. However, with the introduction of sound economic policies such as the free market, free trade, and the forces of globalization, Hong Kong has become a global giant. Great business minds helped to make Hong Kong what it is today. One such person was Li Ka–Shing, who according to *Forbes* is one of the richest men in Asia. His company Cheung Kong Holdings and Hutchison Whampoa controls businesses in manufacturing, steel, telecommunications, energy, real estate and an array of others. He was once described by Louis Kraar of *Fortune* magazine as a man who 'combines the instincts of a gambler with the calculation of an actuary.' Li's philosophy is very simple. He says, 'If you keep a good reputation, work hard, be nice to people, keep your promises, your business will be much easier.' Due to Hong Kong's growth, its stock exchange is the second largest in Asia. The city has one of the most beautiful skylines in the world. The Pritzker Prize-winning Architect I. M. Pei, whose works include the Louvre Pyramid in Paris, has a signature structure on the Hong Kong skyline: The Bank of China Tower in Hong Kong, which is one of the world's most recognizable skyscrapers, is the 4th tallest building in Hong Kong."

"Alex, thanks for educating me. I didn't have the faintest idea that sound economic policies were the reasons for Hong Kong's meteoric rise."

"Well Abdul, now you know. As it has been a long day, let's retire now and pick it up tomorrow afternoon. I am supposed to be in court at 1:30pm so pick me up at 1pm prompt. I will be sharing some insights with you. Have a safe drive home and see you in the afternoon."

CHAPTER FIVE

Courage, A Winner's Best Friend

"My message especially to young people is to have courage to think differently, courage to invent, to travel the unexplored path, courage to discover the impossible and to conquer the problems and succeed."

— A.P. J. Abdul Kalam

"Good day Alex, how are you doing?"

"I am well, thanks. Interestingly enough, my slated court appearance has been postponed to next week, Tuesday. But I would like us to go for lunch, so today, let's eat at *Little Hanoi*, my favourite Vietnamese restaurant in Elephant and Castle. Have you eaten Vietnamese food before?"

"Yes I have Alex, though I've eaten it only once. One of my regular clients, Joan, a ballerina with the English National Ballet invited me for her 30th birthday party. The event was held in a Vietnamese restaurant in Wimbledon. I remember enjoying the food."

"If you enjoyed the food, why haven't you eaten it a few times more?"

"Well Alex, I must confess that I had a fear of introducing new things in my life. Whether it was a new routine, or a new meal. You have no idea how much you have helped me overcome that. Since I met you I can't even count how many new things I have introduced in my life. Reading, running, attending comedy shows, praying, meditation, drinking lots of water, eating new foods—even the way I dress has changed. I can't thank you enough for all you have done for me. Abdul, like I have said several times, your desire to see change and your hunger fueled me."

"I also want to thank you for being a fabulous student. You have equally been a blessing to me.

"You know I have talked a lot about visiting Scandinavia to learn some principles in helping you build a great business or nation. From my suggestions you may think that these countries are perfect and do not face any problems. That is far from it. No country on this earth is perfect, because man is imperfect and lives in an imperfect world. Every country has challenges, even Switzerland or my beloved Norway.

"Let me give you some examples. The cost of living in Norway is astronomical. I remember once meeting a Norwegian when I was in Paris. We got to talking about Norway, since I told her it's a country I absolutely love. She was a CEO of a major corporation. She lamented about the cost of living and how high her taxes were. According to her she was taxed about 50 percent of her income. She had a son and said she would have possibly had two more children if it weren't that expensive to raise a child. Now if a CEO of a major corporation was lamenting about the cost of living, just imagine it for the ordinary citizen, who is not as well paid as this CEO.

"Switzerland is another example. I was in Zurich some years ago and per my usual practice, went on a tour of the city. On the tour the knowledgeable guide gave me so much history about this beautiful city. On thing she said however, which got me thinking, was the fact that only about 37% of the Swiss owned their homes. Meaning nearly 63% of Swiss rented their homes. This sounded awful to me. She explained that the reason is two-fold. Firstly this is because a large number of residents—about 25%—are foreigners, but also because prices of homes are an arm and a leg, so people could not afford them. I could go on and on about the challenges faced by all the countries I have visited to date. But you get the point, so these two examples are enough.

"Economics is a subject I am interested in. So I am constantly studying it. For you who wants to be President and initiate sound economic policies, I will recommend that you thoroughly study this subject. Adam Smith in 1776 observed that the inland parts of Africa and Asia were the least economically developed areas in the world. This meant that a country's geographical location can be a barrier to prosperity, and that landlocked countries are generally more disadvantaged than non-landlocked countries. In the early 2000s this theory became even more popular. In an article titled 'Challenges Facing Landlocked Developing Countries' published in the *Journal of Human Development*, Michael L. Faye, John W. McArthur, Jeffrey D. Sachs, and Thomas Snow went further. They enumerated reasons that landlocked countries are disadvantaged, because of poor transport systems, i.e., waterways to export their products, and due to which can be doomed to fail.

"Many examples of these categories of countries are found in Sub-Saharan Africa. Countries such as Mali, Niger, Chad, Democratic Republic of Congo, Malawi, Burundi and more. This theory is accepted by many. However, if this theory was entirely true, then Switzerland stood no chance of being a developed country, because as you may already know, Switzerland is landlocked.

"And Switzerland isn't the only landlocked country in Europe. Austria, Czech Republic, Hungary, and a host of others are all landlocked.

"I also argue that if Germans, for example, moved to Niger, in a maximum of 30 years, Niger would be a developed country and geography would certainly have nothing to do with this transformation. Germans are doers: they are solution-oriented and simply get things done.

"Abdul, learn from renowned economists, but you should always challenge what you are learning. I will say that that there are other reasons why these countries are not developing as fast as they should and geography would be the least of my reasons. In the future, after I have studied a lot more about Africa and visited some countries to learn more, then we will explore this topic in more detail."

CHAPTER SIX

Woman You Are An Agent of Change

"Women like men should try and do the impossible. And when they fail, their failure should be a challenge to others."

— Amelia Earhart

On another day, the lessons continued.

"Hello Abdul, how are you doing? Jean and the children send their regards.

"How are they all doing Alex?"

"They are in top form and making progress every day. Oftentimes I am in awe over how I became this fortunate. To have a supportive wife and children who are thriving is a great blessing. I must say though that I work very hard to make these relationships work. As I said earlier, harmony in marriage won't fall in one's lap. You have to work at it daily. Sometimes though, I wish we had a daughter. If I had a daughter, I would have raised her just as I am raising my sons. To be confident, resourceful, diligent, kind, bold—the list is endless.

"Jean and I have been fantasizing lately again about adopting a girl. We will see how far we take this idea. Since you have two adorable girls, I will like to share with you stories of very successful women. Woman who made history in the arts, science, technology, business and other fields. With others making history in their industry, women have realized that they can and should use all the talents and gifts God has bestowed on them. I will give you a variety of examples dating as far back as the 16th century. I could take you even centuries before that if I were to talk about Wu Zetian, the Emperor of China who ruled for 15 years during the Zhou and Tang dynasties many hundreds of years ago.

"So the achievements of women go many centuries back. Various political regimes, empires, and I dare say religious groups tried in the past to suppress women and paint a picture that women were somehow inferior, unintelligent and must be cordoned off to the backstage of life. However I can tell you sincerely that in the beginning it was not so. In the beginning God said, *Let us make mankind (male and female) in our image and after our likeness and let them (male and female) have complete authority over the fish of the sea, the birds of the air, the beasts and over all of the earth and over everything that creeps upon the earth. So God created man in his own image, in the image and likeness of God he created him; male and female he created them. And God blessed them (male and female) and said to them, be fruitful, multiply, and fill the earth, and subdue it (using all its vast resources in the service of God and man), and have dominion over the fish of the sea, the birds of the air, and over every living creature that moves upon the earth.'*

"From this passage it is obvious that God commanded both male and female to have dominion over creation. There is nothing here suggesting that females are weak, inferior or stupid. Since you have girls, it is very important to put in their periphery influential female role models as well as male role models. Hang pictures of successful people on a wall in your home. This will reinforce the fact that they are supposed to contribute significantly to their world.

"The saying that you become what you see is undeniable. Before the British athlete and physician Roger Bannister ran under 4 miles per minute on a mild summer day in May 1954 on the Iffley Road track in Oxford, it was assumed that no human being could run that fast. Once he set that record, he opened the floodgates for others to run through. Believe it or not, his record lasted only 45 days. John Landy shattered his record on the 46th day. Belief and the ability to see change is powerful. But let's turn to powerful women."

Look at Mae C. Jemison, a physician and NASA astronaut. Mae was born in Alabama in October 1956. At the age of 3, her entire family moved to Chicago, where her parents knew she would be better educated and have better opportunities. She had a keen interest in science and nature. Whenever she was asked what she wanted to become in the future, her answer was always, 'I want to be a scientist.' When she was 16 she enrolled in Stanford University in California to study Chemical Engineering.

One of her inspirations for striving for success was Dr. Martin Luther King. "Too often people paint him like Santa—smiley and inoffensive," she said. "But when I think of Martin Luther King, I think of attitude, audacity, and bravery." Even though she felt mistreated by some lecturers because of her race and gender, she persevered and didn't give up. She wrote: "Majoring in engineering as a black woman was difficult because race was always an issue in the United States. Some professors would just pretend I wasn't there. I would ask a question and a professor would act as if it was just so dumb, the dumbest question he had ever heard. Then, when a white guy would ask the same question, the professor would say, 'That's a very astute observation.'"

She then pursued further studies at Cornell Medical School, obtaining a doctorate degree in Medicine in 1981. In 1987, she applied to NASA's astronaut programme for the second time and was selected. She worked in various capacities in NASA and on September 12, 1992, she became the first African American woman to travel in space when she went into orbit aboard the space shuttle Endeavour. "The first thing I saw from space was Chicago, my hometown," said Jemison. "I was working on the middeck where there aren't many windows, and as we passed over Chicago, the commander called me up to the flight deck. It was such a significant moment because since I was a little girl I had always assumed I would go into space."

Jemison was in space for 190 hours, 30 minutes, 23 seconds. Because of her contribution to science, Jemison has been awarded nine honorary doctorates in science, engineering, letters, and the humanities from institutions such as Dartmouth College and Princeton University.

The next outstanding woman is the Venetian philosopher Elena Lucrezia Cornaro Piscopia. Elena was born on 5 June 1646 in Venice, Italy. By the tender age of seven, Elena began studying Latin and Greek. She also studied Hebrew, Spanish, French, and Arabic, becoming a polyglot in the process. In her later years, her studies included mathematics, philosophy, and theology. In June 1678 she became the first woman to receive a doctoral degree from a university, having been conferred a Doctor in Philosophy from the University of Padua. She was highly revered throughout Europe due to her academic prowess. She later became a mathematics lecturer in this university.

The final extraordinary woman for today is Charlotte Cooper Sterry. Charlotte was born in September 1870 in Ealing, Middlesex.

At a very young age, she learnt to play tennis and had very good coaches. With their help, she won her first senior singles title when she was 23 years old. At the age of 26, she became deaf, but she didn't give up her dreams. Between 1893 and 1917, Charlotte participated in 21 Wimbledon tournaments and won five singles Grand Slam titles. On 11 July 1900 she became not only the first female to win an Olympic gold medal but she also became the first individual female Olympic champion. Because she excelled in her field and set so many records, in 2013 she was inducted into the International Tennis Hall of Fame.

"Now this is what I call success. When she become deaf at 26 years old, she could have wallowed in self-pity and have allowed that situation to derail her already flourishing career but she didn't. We should all learn from Charlotte. You must not allow life's circumstances to destroy the vision you have. After winning the Olympics she gave other women the opportunity to compete.

"Abdul, I want to retire now. I need to get home early and prepare for my speech in Edinburgh tomorrow. Please drop me off at Waterloo Station. I will see you when I get back. Send my warm regards to Halima and the girls. Practice all that you are learning from me. Maybe come up with a surprise for Halima. It may be a simple act like taking her out for lunch, taking her to the bookstore, or if she appreciates flowers, buy a bunch for her.

"Some men make the mistake of thinking all women are the same. They assume that every woman appreciates flowers, or jewelry or the softer things of life to feel loved. You will be amazed to learn that not every woman appreciates flowers as a means of communicating affection. For some a ticket to participate in an extreme sport, or to go hiking or to have a lot of sex when she wants it communicates such love and affection. Find out what fills Halima's love tank up and just do it."

"Wow Alex, thank you very much for this insight. I will surprise her this weekend."

"Abdul, make sure you give her some details of what you are planning so she can look forward to it and if it's an evening date, make arrangements to send the children to some friends or have a nanny come over. Some women need to plan and prepare mentally before a date. Don't misconstrue this as being rigid. Because you don't deal with the kids on a daily basis you may not fully understand what it takes to deal with them full-time. Have you ever been left alone with the children for say, one week?"

"Never Alex. Could I survive that? The longest I have spent with the children without Halima was a weekend. They always go to their grandparents when Halima is travelling."

"Trust me Abdul, you will survive. During that period you will bond with them like never before, and you will also have a firsthand experience of what it is like to raise the kids. You will be thankful for Halima and the contribution she is making. Sometimes we men think that providing the finances for our homes is a more difficult task. You will have a different view after such an experience. If Halima ever wants to pursue a short course where students will be resident on campus I recommend that you willingly say yes."

"Oh Alex, I have a confession to make."

"Tell me Abdul, spill the beans."

"Halima has always wanted to pursue a degree in Engineering at the Open University. Even though it's an online degree, there is a two-week residential school every year. And to be honest, because I would be alone with the children for that length of time I told her to wait until the children are older, say 14 or so. I don't know how I will fare for two whole weeks with the girls alone. And how will I work?"

"Abdul, I can now see why Halima is not as alive as she should be. When you don't allow your spouse to pursue his or her dreams, you kill them unintentionally. They will not be dead physically but they will die inside. Once a person is dead inside you cannot expect them to live a passionate life. For once I will be a little bit harsh toward you. You have not been fair to Halima. You have not treated her highly. You have not supported her. In a nutshell, you have not loved her. You have acted selfishly and not in her best interest. Her indifference is a result of this. She is fighting back in a very subtle way.

"Why would you do this Abdul? Just imagine this same treatment meted out to one of your daughters. Will you be happy about it? Look at the investment you are making in your children, ensuring they are well educated so they can stand on their feet in the future. Will you not be upset that all this investment has gone down the drain if they don't use it in the future? Imagine one of your girls graduating from Oxford University with a Masters Degree in Molecular and Cellular Biochemistry and then wants to pursue a PhD in order to become a researcher in that field or a geneticist? But because she gets married, her husband tells her to put this dream on the back burner for 14 years until after the children are old. How do you think your daughter would react?"

"Oh Alex, I never saw things in this light."

"Now Abdul, one thing you need to know is that children who see both parents achieving at work and in life grow up with the knowledge that they have to pursue their dreams. There is now research backing this. Don't get me wrong, I am not advocating that every woman should be in full-time employment immediately after having a baby. If one can take a few months or years off to nurture their children, then they should, since we know the benefit of a mother bonding with their babies. Also bear in mind that every individual is different so you just have to find out what works for you and for him or her. We all have different levels of tolerating pressure. Some women thrive when they have a lot going on, but some don't do quite as well. And to be honest, Halima wanting to pursue an Engineering degree part-time is not asking for much is it?"

"Alex, thanks for telling me off and saying it exactly as it is. I had no idea she was fighting back silently and this was because I didn't agree to her pursuing a degree. I now know that I have acted selfishly; I will change. When I get home I will apologize to her and tell her to go ahead and apply. If she gains entry, she will start in October. Even though this will be hard on us, since both of us will be studying, I am determined to do this."

"Well, go for it, grace will be given to you to accomplish this. I can imagine the excitement she will feel when you give her this good news. You will both experience a 360-degree turnaround in your relationship. The new Halima will amaze you. She will be happier, passionate, and will show you such love. I can't wait to hear how things have turned out for the better. Here is the picture I already see of you both: Abdul the renowned lawyer and President of Ghana, Halima the distinguished civil engineer building bridges and roads in Ghana and beyond. If Halima becomes an active member of your political party, you can actually nominate her for a position in your cabinet. She can be the Minister of Transport or Minister of Roads and Highways. Intelligent women like Ngozi Okonjo-Iweala, Mary Robinson, and Condoleezza Rice have further proved that women, when given the opportunity, will blossom."

"Alex, I appreciate you a thousand times over. You have given me so much to think about. I promise you that from today I will start practicing this. I will see women as God sees them, equal to men. I won't even wait to implement this when I become president of Ghana, I will do this now. And when I set up my law firm I will ensure women are rightly represented. How on earth can I repay you for all you have done for me?"

"Fantastic Abdul, I really look forward to seeing this. And for all you know you will set a record in the UK as the law firm with the highest number of competent female partners. To be honest, God would not have created women if he didn't think they were equally as important as men.

"Abdul, let's continue this conversation when we next meet in two days. Pick me up at the same time."

CHAPTER SEVEN

Take the Bull by the Horns

"The starting point of all achievement is desire."

— Napoleon Hill

"And how is Abdul faring today?"

"I am in very high spirits Alex."

"Wow, give me the good news then. I'm all ears."

"When I got home the other day, I told Halima I wanted to have a discussion with her once she put the children to bed. She grunted and said she was tired and wanted to sleep. In the past I would have reacted, but I kept my cool knowing that I had some exciting news for her. She then sat down and folded her arms, making eye contact with the ceiling and not with me.

"I then held her hands and went on my knees. You should have seen the shock on her face. These are the exact words I said:

'Halima, I am very sorry for treating you this way for the last five years. To be frank, I haven't treated you as my equal: I have been selfish at times, and interested in promoting my agenda alone. In certain instances, I have not respected your opinions, neither have I given you room to operate. This is especially true in regards to you wanting to pursue a degree with the Open University. I am very sorry for saying no to you. Firstly, I didn't see the need in you pursuing this degree. Actually, I didn't know that this degree was key to you becoming all that God created you to be. Please find it in your heart to forgive me. Going forward things in our home will be different.'

'How different?' Halima asked.

'First of all I will want you to apply for your degree today so you can start school in October once you are selected. Immediately you start school, I will relieve you of some chores at home. I will employ a housekeeper who will come in twice a week to clean the house and wash our laundry. I will also be in charge of our weekly grocery shopping. I will either go to the supermarket myself or order it online so it will be delivered.

'Secondly, I will do everything in my power to ensure you graduate with a first-class education. I will get you to attend seminars, workshops, and talks delivered by renowned engineers. I will also find ways to get you connected with eminent professors in other universities. Teachers who will help you better understand engineering.

She said, 'And how will we pay for all of this considering we are tight on cash at the moment and you will also be going back to school?'

'Well, I have thought about it and I am proposing that we either remortgage our home if we want to continue living here in East Ham or sell this house and move to the outskirts of London like Purfleet or Grays so we can raise some cash to fund all of this.'

"Now Alex, the next thing I heard was a very loud cry.

"This startled me so I asked, 'What's the matter Halima?'

"Then the sobbing really began. Halima cried for nearly an hour. Had the children not been asleep they may have thought that I may have said something cruel to their mum.

"When her tears finally dried up, we continued the conversation.

"She told me she was on the verge of running away. That she was planning to run away to Senegal. She is Senegalese, you know. Apparently she had been saving religiously for this trip. Her plan was to bolt with the children on one of the weekends when I would be working in Manchester. I couldn't believe what I was hearing. So here I was thinking that life was normal. Only to discover to my horror that things were not normal in my home. I would have had the biggest shock in my life."

"Abdul, some men fail to realize that some women are different in this regard. Some women could have a storm brewing inside them and nothing on the exterior will show. Perhaps she would have been complaining or trying to get your attention for a while. If these attempts failed to yield any changes she would then start cooking up a plan. Which can be destructive. Truthfully, no marriage disintegrates because of a single argument or problem. There usually would be unresolved issues for years and then one day, a 'seemingly tiny incident' blows it apart."

"You are right, because the last time Halima mentioned this subject of school was about two years ago. After I gave her my long lecture on why I thought it was not feasible at the time she never uttered a word. Since she never raised the topic, I assumed she understood my point of view. Little did I know it was otherwise.

"I then went on to tell her how much I loved her and how much I wanted her to succeed as an individual. I also reiterated that I will respect her views and will always solicit her input on matters concerning us, and that she was the most important person in my life. When I uttered those words it was like a light bulb went on inside her. Her next action stunned me even more. She grabbed me and gave me the most long, wet and passionate kiss I can ever remember receiving from her. Honestly, I was so taken unawares that initially I just stood there, but after about 10 seconds I got right into it and yes, there were fireworks, just like the fireworks ignited on Sydney Harbour Bridge at midnight on the 1st of January. It was heavenly.

"Halima is now a completely different woman. In the last 24 hours, I have been the happiest husband in the world. Alex, thank you for saving my marriage."

"Abdul, I can see the voluminous smile on your face and your buoyancy. I am grateful for this turnaround in your relationship. I have no doubt that it is God at work. I also want to commend you for being a willing vessel that God could use. Frankly, you could have chosen to ignore all the input I made and without even trying, assume the advice I had given wouldn't work for you. I find this with some people I have taught in the past. They never used what I taught them and are still in the same predicament 5 or 10 years on. When I met one of them in particular after 12 years away, his situation hadn't changed. He was still as miserable as sin.

"You have made me so happy today Abdul. For all your hard work and desire to see change in your family, I have a gift for you. Here you go!"

"Oh wow, Alex I can't believe this! A ticket and hotel reservations for a weekend away in Barcelona? Alex, how did you organize all this considering the fact that I just narrated the story to you?"

"Well Abdul, don't forget I am an old man. I have been around for a long time. You know, I planned all this yesterday. I knew that this would be the reaction you would get if you took my advice. So before we left for Edinburgh, I told Jean to book your tickets via Easyjet and also make your hotel reservation at Royal

Passeig de Gracia Hotel. Jean and I stayed in this luxurious 4-star hotel when we celebrated our 15th wedding anniversary. Barcelona is a city you will love. You should indulge in Catalan cuisine and the hundreds of tapas bars that dot the city. The architecture in Barcelona is like no other city in the world.

"The Sagrada Familia especially is a building that has fascinated me for years. I have always been intrigued by its design. The first time Jean and I saw it, we wondered how on earth a 170-meter building could look like this. At first glance, it looks like a building a 10-year-old child would construct. Possibly with Lego bricks, clay, or Play-Doh. But a closer look reveals something different. This building is made of stone—I mean real stone, Abdul.

"The Sagrada Familia is nothing like you have ever seen. It is different, imposing, bodacious, avant-garde, and has no straight lines. If I were asked to describe the Sagrada in one or two words (even though I will struggle to do that), I would say it is an architectural phenomenon, a monument you must see in your lifetime. During one trip to Barcelona, we visited this magnificent cathedral four times. Even though the Sagrada Familia is still under construction, it is the most visited monument in the whole of Spain. This cathedral is expected to be completed in 2030 and is funded by money from the sale of entry tickets and private donors who are anonymous. In 2009 alone the budget was EURO18m. Seven of Antoni Gaudi's works are UNESCO World Heritage Sites. Now just to put this in context, so you can see how celebrated this genius is, Ghana and Nigeria have two UNESCO World Heritage Sites each and Malaysia has four.

"Antoni Gaudi was a religious man, so he even earned the nickname 'God's Architect.'

"To get into the mind of Gaudi the architect, we went on a guided architectural tour which showcased his other great works, like Park Güell, Casa Batlló and Casa Mila among others. During the tour, it was evident that Gaudi lived by some principles, which were highlighted after the tour. To say we were inspired after learning about Gaudi and his work would be an understatement. Jean and I were determined to inculcate into our own lives the principles this great architect lived by. Even though Gaudi died over 88 years ago, his philosophy is still relevant today. The first principle Gaudi lived by was *purpose*—Gaudi didn't see himself as an ordinary architect merely designing buildings. He felt he was an instrument in God's hands sent to earth to create great works. This is best captured in his own words: 'In the Sagrada Familia, everything is providential'

"Secondly, Gaudi was *focused*. He concentrated on his work so much that he was often described as being a loner and unsociable. He certainly wasn't a person who engaged in chitchat or mindless conversations. Thirdly, Gaudi *worked* like a maniac. He spent over 12 hours a day working on the Sagrada. Fourthly, he was an *original*. Prior to the buildings he created, there was no architectural style like his. Gaudi fused Neo-gothic architecture, Art Nouveau, Oriental techniques, and an organic style inspired by nature. This magnificent cathedral has no straight lines. He is quoted as saying: *'Those who look for the laws of Nature as a support for their new works collaborate with the creator.'* Gaudi rarely drew detailed plans of his works. He preferred to create them as three-dimensional scale models and mold the details as he conceived them.

"Fifthly, Gaudi *believed in himself* and in his ideas. That was why he had the courage to design a building like this. If he didn't believe his work would become the most visited-monument in Spain he would not have dared to invent a new architectural style. Sixtly, Gaudi was fully *committed* to this project. From 1883 till 7th June 1926 (when he was knocked down by a tram and died 3 days later), he lived and breathed the Sagrada. He was also remarkably detailed. Gaudi personally oversaw the detailing of all the sculptures, ceramic, stained glass, iron forging and carpentry work on the cathedral. The sheer number of sculptures on the Passion Facade alone is enough to make you stand in awe. I remember standing at this section for one full hour without moving.

"And lastly, Gaudi saw *The Big Picture*. When he became involved with the Sagrada in 1883, he knew that he wouldn't be around to see its completion. He actually predicted that the cathedral would take 200 years to build. But thanks to technology, this has been halved. Even though he knew that other architects would carry on with the project he was willing to 'share his recognition' with others. Now that is what I call genius. Gaudi's influence extends beyond the world of architecture."

"Alex, do you know Barcelona was one of the cities I intended visiting with Halima?"

"Really? I never knew. I just chose it because I felt it was a city you would enjoy."

"How on earth can I repay you Alex, for all that you have done for me?"

"Abdul, God will repay me. All you have to do is pray for me. God has in the past sent others to help me too. I always see myself as God's hands and feet.

"Since we have celebrated your victory Abdul, I want to continue sharing about women making history.

"Today I will focus on Hanna Reitsch, the first woman to fly a helicopter, a rocket plane and a jet fighter.

Hanna was born on 29th March 1912 in Jelenia Gora in Poland. Her father, an ophthalmologist, wanted her to become a doctor but Hanna was interested in aviation. While she was in medical school in Berlin, she enrolled in a flying school in Staaken. She eventually left medical school in 1933, as her passion for aviation was more than her love for medicine. Between 1935 and 1957 these are the records Hanna set:

- 1932: women's gliding endurance record (5.5 hours)

- 1936: women's gliding distance record (305 km (190 mi))

- 1937: first woman to cross the Alps in a glider

- 1937: the first woman in the world to be promoted to flight captain, by Colonel Ernst Udet

- 1937: world distance record in a helicopter (109 km (68 mi))

- 1938: the first person to fly a helicopter (Focke-Wulf Fw 61) inside an enclosed space (Deutschlandhalle)

- 1938: winner of German national gliding competition Sylt-Breslau (Silesia)

- 1939: women's world record in gliding for point-to-point flight.

- 1943: while in the Luftwaffe, the first woman to pilot a rocket plane (Messerschmitt Me 163). She survived a disastrous crash, though with severe injuries, and because of this she became the first and only German woman to receive the Iron Cross 1st Class.

- 1944: the first woman in the world to pilot a jet aircraft at the Luftwaffe research centre at Rechlin during the trials of the Messerschmitt Me 262 and Heinkel He 162

- 1952: third place in the World Gliding Championships in Spain together with her teammate Lisbeth Häfner

- 1955: German gliding champion

• 1956: German gliding distance record (370 km (230 mi))

• 1957: German gliding altitude record (6,848 m (22,467 ft)

"Hanna was such a successful pilot that the first president of Ghana, Dr. Kwame Nkrumah, invited her to set up a flying school in Ghana. A challenge she took on. With funding from the West German government, the Afienya gliding school in Ghana was born."

"What, Alex—do you mean this lady set up the Afienya gliding school?"

"Yes I do."

"Alex, to be honest I never knew this story and I don't think many Ghanaians know this either."

"Abdul, history is very important. Whenever you visit a country, or library or park, take it upon yourself to find out how that place came into being. You will be amazed at how knowledgeable you will become by taking this simple approach to learning. I developed my learning muscle this way. Often times the choice of cities I visit is based on its history or a store or library I may have read about. A typical example is A Coruña in the Galician region of Spain. I personally know scores of people who visit Spain often. But I can count the number of people I know who have been to A Coruña.

"I decided to visit this city after reading Covadonga O'Shea's book *The Man From Zara: the Story of the Genius Behind the Inditex Group* and learning that the first store of the clothing chain Zara is located here. Reading about Amancio Ortega and the unconventional way he built this mammoth company while remaining almost anonymous in the process baffled me. How could one of the richest men in the world be this hidden?

"Alex, your depth and breadth of knowledge is beyond belief. How on earth does a surgeon know all this?"

"Well, with mentors like Benjamin Franklin, Thomas Jefferson, and Isaac Newton I had no choice other than to become a student for life. With the knowledge they acquired in their lifetime, they have proven that we humans have the capacity to grow our minds. If we only all believed this.

"Have you read the newspapers or watched the news in the last two days?"

"No I haven't Alex," I said. "I have been too busy reading and I have turned my car into a university on wheels, so I haven't had any time to even listen to the news."

"Well, I thought I'd let you know that the verdict for my trial will be given today."

"What? Today?"

"Well," Alex continued, "This means that after today, I will either be sent to prison or I will return to my normal life, where I will take the train or buses."

"Oh my goodness!" I exclaimed. "What is going to happen to me, Alex?"

Just then, tears started pouring down my cheeks. I couldn't believe my time with Alex was coming to an end. Who would inspire me? Who would look out for me? Who would show me such unconditional love?

"Abdul, I understand how you feel. But please don't act like you will never see me for the rest of your life. I will still be there to help you. However, with the tools I have already given you, you will be on your way to success. I have no doubt that you will thrive. I will have a meeting with you once every quarter to help and monitor your progress. I am with you in this forever. Your success and joy will be mine too. I want to see you flourish and become all you were created to be. I want to see you happy every single day of your life."

"Alex, before you carry on, I want to let you know that meeting you has changed my life, in ways beyond measure. In the past few weeks, I realized that I needed to make many significant changes in my life in order to achieve all the dreams I had as a teenager. I sat down a few days ago and wrote my goals for the next 15 years. I want to share them with you.

1. Enroll for a law degree with the Open University
2. Go on a date every Friday with Halima
3. Learn Mandarin and French
4. Take a six-month photography course
5. Read two books a month
6. Travel to Helsinki with Halima and the girls
7. Volunteer at a drug rehabilitation shelter once a week
8. Learn to cook so I can cook at home
9. Invest GBP100 every month
10. Attend a course on personal development every year
11. Set up a law firm in the UK and establish branches in Ghana, Kenya and South Africa
12. Exercise three times a week
13. Pray and meditate every day
14. Spend at least an hour a day with the children
15. Fund schooling for two underprivileged children

"Wow Abdul, I am humbled by your goals! I am beside myself with joy. I believe you will achieve all these within the time frame you have stated. Well done. I am very proud of you!

"Finally Abdul, I would like to give you *The Invitation* by Oriah Mountain Dreamer. It is a poem that cuts through the noise and gets into your heart. It is a poem that causes you to ask the deep questions that tug at your heart. It is a poem that may make you cry, but has the potential to make you laugh—if you live your authentic life."

He handed me the book to read. I have it here, and here is how the poem goes:

It doesn't interest me what you do for a living. I want to know what you ache for, and if you dare to dream of meeting your hearts longing.

It doesn't interest me how old you are. I want to know if you will risk looking like a fool for love, for your dreams, for the adventure of being alive.

It doesn't interest me what planets are squaring your moon. I want to know if you have touched the center of your own sorrow, if you have been opened by life's betrayals, or have become shriveled and closed from fear of further pain.

I want to know if you can sit with pain, mine or your own, without moving to hide it or fade it or fix it. I want to know if you can be with joy, mine or your own; if you can dance with wildness and let the ecstasy fill you to the tips of your fingers and toes without cautioning us to be careful, be realistic, or to remember the limitations of being human.

It doesn't interest me if the story you are telling me is true, I want to know if you can disappoint another to be true to yourself. if you can bear the accusation of betrayal and not betray your own soul.

I want to know if you can be faithful and therefore trustworthy. I want to know if you can see beauty, even when it is not pretty every day, and if you can source your life from its presence.

I want to know if you can live with failure, yours or mine, and still stand on the edge of a lake and shout to the silver of the full moon,

"Yes!"

It doesn't interest me to know where you live or how much money you have. I want to know if you can get up after the night of grief and despair, weary and bruised to the bone, and do what needs to be done for the children.

It doesn't interest me who you are, or how you came to be here- I want to know if you will stand in the center of the fire with me and not shrink back.

It doesn't interest me where or what or with whom you have studied I want to know what sustains you from the inside when all else falls away. I want to know if you can be alone with yourself, and if you truly like the company you keep in the empty moments.

After reading it, I was sobbing like a baby. Alex couldn't hold back his tears too. We both cried and cried and cried.

When I finished sobbing, Alex just looked at me and said, "I love you Abdul. I wish the very best for you. I pray that you will implement all the lessons I have shared with you.

"I pray you live an authentic life. A life of purpose, passion, joy, kindness, forgiveness, charity, and adventure; a life truly worth living. May you be the light of the world, a city on a hill. May you never be hidden.

"Until our next meeting it's farewell for now."

A part of me wanted to go to the Royal Courts of Justice to hear the final verdict. However I wasn't myself, so I decided to go home early and watch the news instead. As it was a high-profile case, I had no doubt it would be on every news channel. At exactly 6:05pm it was declared that Alex Bond was acquitted of negligence in the case brought against him by the family of Alfred Simons. The relief I felt could not be described in words. Alex had been vindicated.

SECTION 2

Photos to Reflect Upon and Inspire

In between the tale of Abdul before and Abdul after, enjoy these photos from my travels. May they free your imagination, and make it move (and may your body follow).

Paddling over Lake Bunyonyi – Uganda

Bungee jumping off Auckland Harbour Bridge – New Zealand

Columbus, The European Space Agency's Science Lab in Space – The Netherlands

The Flame of Hope at the Kigali Genocide Memorial – Rwanda

The Royal Danish Library, aka Black Diamond, Copenhagen - Denmark

Attending a Maori Concert – New Zealand

Celebrating on the Sand Dunes in Sossusvlei – Namibia

The Spectacular Norwegian Fjords – Norway

Giant Aldabra Tortoises, Prison Island, Zanzibar - Tanzania

Sydney Harbour Bridge, Sydney - Australia

Climbing Table Mountain, Cape Town - South Africa

With a bagpipe player, Edinburgh - UK

SECTION 3

This section is the recounting of further conversations between Abdul and Alex, with a huge difference: Abdul and Alex are together again, but many years later. It is early summer of 2015, and Abdul's life has been utterly galvanized by what he learned from Alex. The two friends have a chance to share warm stories of their respective life paths. I felt privileged (and inspired) to hear of them and to marvel at my friend Abdul's happy success.

CHAPTER EIGHT

Rock the Boat
At All Cost

"Success seems to be connected with action. Successful people keep moving. They make mistakes but they don't quit."

— Conrad Hilton

"Alex, my encounter with you was the beginning of my transformation. Had it not been for you, I am sure I would have remained an average human being, working in an average job, and spending time with friends going nowhere.

"After our first conversation years ago, I put my life in order. The first thing I did was that I completely cut off my negative friends and started making friends with intelligent, positive, determined, and passionate people. I came to understand that, as you said, I would become what I see.

"Secondly, I actively began working on my goals. I enrolled with the Open University to pursue a law degree. I graduated with an LLM, then moved on to the vocational stage of training, after which I qualified as a solicitor. During my professional training I met Jeremy Suppey, who had graduated from Oxford Law School a few years earlier. We become friends and realized our visions and dreams were in sync, so we decided to set up a law firm, Dinnani, Suppey and Partners.

"My date nights with Halima are embossed in my diary. I make sure I stick to them, never allowing any meeting to derail them, unless I am out of the country. Even when that happens I make it up as soon as I return. I came to the realization that it was whole-heartedly worth pursuing a healthy, wholesome and enjoyable marriage. After all, my family is the most important aspect of my life. Nothing can compare with the value of my family. And I took the photography course, and prayed every day.

"Alex, the journey was not easy: I remember the months I failed to save the GBP100 a month when I was in school, or the months things were not going 100% right with Halima, and I felt discouraged and wanted to give up. But during those dark days, I remembered your words about pressing on, no matter the circumstances or seasons of life. Now I can say without a shadow of doubt that this journey had been worth pursuing. On some days I wake up and wonder if this person is me. I am living a brand new life.

"Our law firm Dinnani, Suppey & Partners is doing marvelously well. We have 4 senior partners, 10 junior partners, and 8 support staff. We recently won some landmark contracts with HSBC, two private equity firms, and one of the world's largest property developers. We are very active in the nonprofit space as well. We deal with issues like disability rights, injustice meted out to prisoners, and child trafficking. Between all the lawyers, we offer 60 hours of pro bono work every month, making our firm, though very small, one of the largest contributors of pro bono work in the world. I believe without a shadow of doubt that I have been raised up to raise others up. I have been placed in this position to alleviate the suffering of others. Life cannot just be about me, myself and I."

"Wow Abdul," he joked, "60 hours of pro bono work a month? This is unbelievable, considering your puny size."

"Alex, you have to meet Jeremy Suppey the co-founder of our law firm. He is one of the brightest young men I know.

"Before we set up our firm, we decided that we were going to have an equal number of women as partners in our organization. In our research we found out that Norway was a leader in gender equality. Ansgar Gabrielsen is a person who spearheaded this very important legislation. In 2002 Gabrielsen, who was serving as Norway's Secretary of Trade and Industry, proposed that all public companies in Norway ensure that at least 40% of their board directors should be women. At the time he made this proposal, there were over 400 publicly listed Norwegian firms who did not have a single female on their board of directors. In an interview Ansgar granted to the British newspaper *The Guardian*, he said:

'The law was not about getting equality between the sexes; it was about the fact that diversity is a value in itself, that it creates wealth. I could not see why after 25–30 years of having an equal ratio of women and men in universities and with having so many educated women with experience, they were few of them on boards. From my time in the business world, I saw how board members were picked: they came from the same small circle of people. They go hunting and fishing together, they are buddies.'

"When he suggested this, he was attacked from all corners. Politicians, business leaders, and even women attacked him. Would you believe his own party opposed this law?

"He was told on many occasions that his proposal was radical and that implementing this law would collapse the economy. Because he proposed that this quota should be a voluntary measure, after three years it made only a 3% gain. So in 2005 the Norwegian government introduced official legislation. This stated that by 1st January 2008, all public companies in Norway were obliged to ensure that at least forty percent of their board directors were women. The Norwegian government made it clear that firms that didn't comply with this directive would be severely punished.

"Any firm that failed to meet this deadline would first pay a heavy fine, then would be de-registered from the Oslo Stock Exchange and finally it would be dissolved. This sent a strong warning, so all public companies started looking for competent women to be on their boards. Currently in Norway women hold over 40% directorships, the highest proportion in the world. When you compare this figure with other European countries you will be amazed at how far Norway has come. In other European countries women make up only 10% of company boards.

"Now Alex, what startled me about Ansgar Gabrielsen was that a Minister of Trade and Industry made this recommendation, not a Minister of Gender and Equality. Also, the fact that a man was championing this cause was remarkable. He was a very wise and courageous man in my opinion. I use the word courageous because he was championing a course that even his party opposed. But like all things that benefit humankind, God's presence is in the background, whether it is abolishing slavery like Abraham Lincoln fought for or fighting against apartheid, like Nelson Mandela did."

"You should learn from this example Abdul. When you become president your party may not always support your decisions, but you should go ahead nonetheless once you know they are decisions that will benefit humankind and advance the course of justice. Oh yes, that I know now. I have also grown to accept that no matter what you do, not everyone will support you. Some people will criticize you."

"Alex, when you suggested that I visit Scandinavia when I met you years ago, I took on the challenge and I can tell you that I fell in love with the whole region. I spent a month each in Norway, Finland, Sweden and Iceland, and three months in Denmark.

"When I was in Oslo in Norway, I visited the Nobel Peace Center and the City Hall where the Nobel Prizes are awarded. I also took the scenic train from Oslo to Bergen. That train journey is the most picturesque train journey I have ever taken. Seeing the majestic Norwegian fjords just melted my heart.

"Alex, had it not been the fact that I know I am called to live in Ghana, I would emigrate to Norway. Nature is truly beautiful. The eye-catching scenery, the healthy quality of life, first-class infrastructure, a premier healthcare system, a very clean environment and other qualities made me fall in love with Norway. Norway is a forward-thinking nation. A nation which gives equal opportunity to both men and women. A nation which reminds me every day that God created both male and female, and he made them equal.

"Since my visit to Norway, my interest in that country has increased. I learnt so many lessons I will surely implement in Ghana when I become President. Recently, the 2015 World Happiness Report was published by the United Nations. It was spearheaded by Jeffery Sachs, economist and Director of the Earth Institute at Columbia University. In the report on happiness, Norway ranked 4th in the world. I wasn't surprised at all by that ranking.

"Thanks to Ansgar Gabrielson and all that we learned about gender equality, Dinnani, Suppey and Partners today have a 47% representation of women, making our firm the most gender-balanced law firm in the whole of the United Kingdom. We have won awards because of this. We have a child-friendly working environment and give 4 extra weeks maternity leave, in addition to the statutory maternity leave of 52 weeks. A partner in one of the largest law firms in the country cornered me a few months ago at an event and said he was in discussion with their board about sending their human resource director to meet with us and learn from us.

"They want to know our secret in running our organization. Especially with regards to how we are this profitable despite giving the extra time off to our female staff. In his firm, only 3% of its partners are women. I simply smiled and told them we will be more than happy to help them. I am thankful to be an example in this light. I can't believe that some years ago I was just wondering on this earth with no vision or goals and no traits of a bright future.

"What I have also started doing since the beginning of this year is mentoring a group of 16-year-old boys from one of the underperforming schools in Essex who are dabbling in alcohol and drugs. I meet with them once a month, challenging them to be all they were created to be. I remember the days I drank excessively. I drank not because I was 'bad' per se but because I was lonely, bored and wanted to be accepted. My strategy in teaching them is not curriculum-based; after reading Guy Claxton's *What's the Point of School? Rediscovering the Heart of Education*, I could clearly see why they were struggling. So our leaning methods are based on what Guy calls 'the eight magnificent qualities.' These are curiosity, courage, exploration, experimentation, imagination, reasoning, sociability and reflection. I try to expose them to different facets of life.

"The disciplines we learn about are varied: from aviation to medicine to relationships, to animals to engineering, to botany, business, architecture, sports, and character development. I remember our first practical lesson on aviation. We went on a tour to the airport and were fortunate enough to be given access to a cockpit. One of the boys, 16-year-old Luke, had never been to the airport before, let alone close to a plane. After that trip, his fascination with aviation has reached a level that has astounded even me. He now wants to be a pilot. The amazing thing too is that his grades in school have improved and he has found a focus he never had. He is now very passionate and talks endlessly about planes. Because of this passion, the principal of his school had to upgrade their school library with books on aviation. If he continues like this, I know he will make waves in the aviation industry in the future."

"Abdul, I am in awe of who you have become and what you have achieved. It is humbling to see how all your experiences, the good, the bad, and the ugly have meshed so well to create your well roundedness. *I am reminded that all things work together for good for those who love God and who are called according to his purpose.* Your future is very bright: I can see you gain recognition for all you are doing and who knows, you might just be recognized by the Queen, like me."

"Well I am sure about that Alex, because within a few months, I will be moving back to Accra, to spearhead our Africa expansion.

"We will open two other offices in Nairobi and Cape Town. Once I move to Accra I will start laying the blocks for my political career. Halima has made significant progress too. She completed her Engineering degree and has been working with one of the leading civil engineering firms. When we move to Accra she will set up a civil engineering firm."

"Abdul, I want to congratulate you for coming this far. When we met years ago I told you that I believed in you and had complete faith in what you would achieve. Thank you for proving me right.

"In the last few years, so many marvelous things have happened to us too. The health facility in Antananarivo has been completed so our team has been spending a lot of time in Madagascar. We have conducted scores of successful operations. I don't spend as much time in St. Thomas Hospital like I used to. The boys are grown up now. My eldest son Caleb has completed university and is currently traveling through Asia. He is keen in shipping and wants to establish a shipping business. While in Asia he will work with a shipping firm in Singapore and Hong Kong. Hopefully when he returns in two years he will be ready to set up a shipping business—well, only if he returns. For all we know he may settle in Asia.

"My second son Paul who was suffering from Down Syndrome is now a violinist. Astonishingly, he was miraculously healed five years ago. He then studied music in Leipzig Germany and currently lives in London. Adrian and Nigel are the only ones at home. They are also doing marvelously in school. Jean has opened an art gallery in London. She also runs exhibitions in various parts of the world. In two months she will be holding an exhibition in a gallery in New York alongside the Chinese artist Ai Weiwei. Our lives have taken amazing turns for which we are grateful."

"Alex, you all have made momentous progress too. I am so proud of you and thankful for how far you have all come. Wow, this is great news!"

"Abdul, do you remember I told you that I had plans of travelling in Africa? Well those dreams have been fulfilled too. In the past year, I have visited over 15 countries in Africa and have learnt so many things I would like to share with you. These will be beneficial to you as an individual and also as you prepare to run for president. Since you are moving back to Ghana, I will encourage you to visit as many countries in Africa as you can.

"The African continent has stupendous potential. Abundant natural resources, a youthful population, arable land, a conducive climate—the list is endless. However, so many factors limit its development and growth. During my time traveling, and all the study I have undertaken about the histories of many African countries, here are some of the observations I have made which I think account for the slow development in many of the countries in Africa. Before I enumerate the reasons, I want to categorically say that not every African exhibits these traits. I have personally met and read about various people making a difference on the continent. For example, Professor PLO Lumumba, Director of The Kenya School of Law, who fights corruption and champions the cause of justice, or the late Professor Dora Akunyili head of

NAFDAC in Nigeria who fought tirelessly to eradicate fake drugs, or the Zambian economist Dambisa Moyo whose book *Dead Aid; Why Aid Is Not Working And How There Is Another Way for Africa* sheds light on the damaging effects aid has had on Africa and gives other alternatives to alleviating poverty, or Ghanaian journalist Anas Aremeyaw Anas whose investigative journalism has brought about change in Ghana or entrepreneur Strive Masiyiwa founder and chairman of Telecom giant Econet Wireless, who advocates doing business without corruption. Strive has used his wealth to provide thousands of scholarships to students through his foundation. There are numerous others contributing immensely to the development of their nations. If I were to name them, we would remain on this subject for the next two months. I also want you to understand that I am not one who sees Africa as most mainstream media portrays it: hunger, destitution, and a war-ravaged continent. Every country in the world can be classified into 4 socio-economic strata based on the citizens' occupation, income, wealth and social status. These 4 levels of classification are the poor, the working class, the middle class and the wealthy or upper class. In all the African countries I have visited to date, I have seen all these 4. So now to my reasons for the snail pace of development in Africa.

• A fixed and negative mindset exhibited by a large number of the populace.

• An absence of effective national institutions like the courts, police and judicial forces

• A lack of education, or education not leading to transformation.

• Not being futuristic in thinking/thinking only about the short term. This is one reason why corruption is king.

• A lack of curiosity in learning and in travelling. There are very few cities in the world I have travelled to where I met other Africans simply travelling to feed their curiosity.

• Not taking ownership, responsibility and initiative for the outcome of their lives. Wanting to blame the government, or witches, or a competitor for any mishap.

• A lack of understanding that no successful business or nation becomes great overnight. As the saying goes, Rome wasn't built in a day. Rome was built daily.

• A belief in magic, witchcraft, and overnight success. A belief that one President coming into power will change the story overnight.

• Preferring not to think and using religion as a cover up.

• Citizens expecting the government to solve all their problems, which include cleaning their homes as well as painting them.

• A lack of leadership.

• Not researching, not questioning or challenging anything. Accepting every doctrine or practice hook, line and sinker.

• A lack of identity. Copying blindly, not being straightforward and always trying to impress others.

• Not documenting knowledge and passing it down to the next generation.

• Greed, greed, and more greed.

Francis Tapon, the Harvard-educated author who is currently travelling around the world by road and has been in Africa since 2013, adds the following to my list above.

• A lack of trust; jealousy.

• Laziness, poor work ethic.

• Men abandoning kids, absent or abusive fathers.

• Extreme tolerance of imperfection and disorder, accepting of lousy situations.

• A chronic tardiness, not understanding the importance of keeping time.

• Tribalism; a disinterest in doing something that improves the wider community, nation, or world.

"This list is depressing, Alex."

"I do agree to an extent, but I think that it is important they are enumerated so you have an understanding of some of the issues you will have to confront when you move back to Ghana. I am telling you these things so you won't become discouraged when you face tribalism or encounter people who want to blame you for all their troubles. Changing a negative mindset that has been entrenched for generations will be tough, but it can be done. And so is eradicating corruption. There are solutions to these challenges. You just need to explore them.

"To bring about change, what I will say is that firstly, you will have to be the example you want to see. If you want to promote cleanliness for example, ensure your own house is clean. The next step might be forming a neighbourhood association whose goal is to be the cleanest area in your city. You should also put in a system of monitoring and measuring this goal. Maybe you can fine anyone seen throwing rubbish away improperly or employ other measures. When you are successful in your area, then you take this message everywhere you go.

"Abdul, a dirty city or country attracts fewer tourists and this definitely impacts the economy. Isn't cleanliness one of the reasons you are attracted to Norway?"

"Of course it is, Alex. Add efficiency and quality infrastructure among the others."

"Abdul, I remember visiting a certain city a while ago. I couldn't wait to leave that place, and I also vowed never to return. You know what drove me out? Filth. That place has certainly lost my tourism income and will lose that income from many more because I told everyone I knew about my horrible experience.

"We should realize that every decision one makes as an individual has an impact on the wider society, whether we accept this or not.

"I know these truths I am sharing with you are not palatable. I am doing so because I am interested in your welfare, and your nation's welfare. People from other parts of the world may be afraid to say these things to you because they may not want to hurt your feelings and possibly be termed racists. Some of them just wish Africans as a whole would get their act together, but others on the other hand just laugh and are convinced things will never change. I have met and read articles by some who argue that blacks are less intelligent than whites. Those purporting this theory are not uneducated. They are well educated in our society. Some are even pioneers who have won Nobel Prizes.

"An example is Dr. James Watson, the winner of the Nobel Prize in 1962. He won the prize for his role in discovering the molecular structure of DNA. In an interview with the *Sunday Times,* he said that he was inherently gloomy about the prospect of Africa 'because all our social policies are based on the fact that their intelligence is the same as ours—whereas all testing says not really'. In the 21st century there is such an interest in DNA that many more theories about intelligence and genetics are being spun and considered.

"Steven Pinker, the professor of psychology, Director of the Center for Cognitive Neuroscience at MIT and author of *The Blank Slate*, argues that genes play the greatest role in shaping humans, so no matter the environment you find yourself, if you were born with 'bad genes' you don't stand a chance of turning out right.

"Of course you and I know that this is not the case, because there is research spanning decades which shows that our environment, culture, education, and upbringing play a huge role in how we turn out as adults. I don't dispute the fact that genes have a role to play in our lives. Genes contribute to our looks and traits, but to say that our genes are solely responsible for the outcome of our lives is untrue. Read Carol Dweck's *Mindset: How You Can Fulfill Your Potential* or Harvard psychologist B. F. Skinner's *Science and Human Behavior*. Some of the reasons for thinking this way are that when annual poverty rankings from institutions such as the World Bank and IMF are published, most of them are in Africa. And also when you visit those countries mentioned in the report, you immediately see the manifestation of the pathologies I enumerated. All these correlate to an absence of basic infrastructure, healthcare, education, high corruption and mismanagement.

"Abdul, let's prove all the critics wrong. Ensure that you build a solid foundation for Ghana to thrive 50 years from today. Now this won't be easy, but remember that nothing sustainable comes easy. If you were to ask Lee Kuan Yew, the first president of Singapore, he will let you know how tough it was to achieve what he did. You would do well to read *From Third World to First* by Lee Kuan Yew and learn how he helped transform Singapore. Also read

A History of Hong Kong by Frank Welsh and *The Miracle: the Epic Story of Asia's Quest for Wealth* by Michael Schuman and learn how Hong Kong, Japan, and South Korea transformed their nations to first-world nations.

"With the level of seriousness and perseverance you have shown, I am confident that you can make it."

"Alex, thanks for having such faith and confidence in me."

"After bombarding you with these truths, I want to share with you an African country that in my opinion is making progress. I am talking about Rwanda.

"Rwanda is a country I was keen to visit. With the history of the genocide and the current progress the country had made, I was eager to understand the driving force behind Rwanda's steady rise.

"When I arrived at Kigali International Airport, I noticed that it was small but squeaky clean. Acquiring my visa at the immigration desk was seamless. I was even given a computerized receipt that clearly stated payment receipt by Rwanda Revenue Authority. This demonstrates Rwanda is serious about building great institutions. Revenue is central in building a successful nation or business so ensuring that all revenue is accounted for is important. The second thing I noticed at the airport was that my bags were not searched when I picked them off the conveyor belt. This is a chronic problem at the airports of most African countries. I have always wondered about the reasoning behind this practice. Abdul, can you imagine the jam which would occur at Terminal 5 in Heathrow Airport if the custom officials wanted to physically search all the bags of incoming passengers?"

"There would be chaos Alex, I can tell you that."

"Oh yes, real chaos and what this will do is simply drive people away. Both business travellers and tourists. Tell me who wants to be asked to open their heavy luggage after a 12-hour flight? The annoying thing too is that when you open your luggage, these officials tend to ask for gifts. I remember being asked for a bottle of perfume from my luggage in your dear country Ghana. I just declined and said it was a gift for a friend."

"Oh Alex, I am ashamed."

"Well, I am telling you these things so you can bring that needed change. When you become president, ban this act. Trust me, it is bad for business and bad for your country. If Rwanda doesn't practice this, then learn from them and do the same.

"The third thing I noticed when I got of the arrival hall was that taxis were neatly arranged outside. I asked a lady at a Forex Bureau just outside the arrivals hall, and she said I should speak to one of the drivers in the blue shirts. When I was approaching, one driver came up to me asking me where I wanted to go. I told him I was going to Kyachiru. He mentioned the fare and off we went.

"Wow, I thought to myself. I didn't get the usual hassle from cab drivers as I normally would in a city like Lagos or Nairobi.

"Abdul, since you were a cab driver, you already know that cab drivers are a source of information and for getting a sense of how a city operates. They have a wealth of knowledge about the restaurants that serve the scrumptious dishes, the cheap areas where you can buy souvenirs and they even sometimes can give you an insight into the political climate of a city.

"Once in the cab I began asking questions about his job, his family, and the changes in Rwanda. He immediately told me he was happy with his job and was optimistic about his future in Rwanda. Because he spoke little English I couldn't get more information from him. I was disappointed, but I knew I would find another taxi driver who would feed me more information. The ride was smooth and easy and certainly traffic free. I noticed how clean the city was, and I definitely didn't see piles of rubbish or plastic bags that usually litter some cities around the world.

"One of the main reasons I decided to visit Rwanda was to gain a better understanding about the genocide and what caused it. So the next day, I jumped on a 'taxi moto' to the Kigali Genocide Memorial. By the way, the museum is free to enable everyone visit it. When I arrived we were ushered in to watch a 10-minute video of the genocide. I nearly broke down during this video. I couldn't fathom what would cause a human being to butcher another human being. Little did I know that the intro video was just a fraction of the drama which would unfold. The harrowing stories were waiting for me in the museum. I went through every room in that building. Two rooms which broke my heart were the children's room and the room with skulls and bones. My goodness.

"Abdul, the children's room had pictures of some of the children who were killed during this period. There were also stories about the children before these atrocious crimes were committed. The foods they liked, how old they were, what their favourite sports were, their ages, and more. Being in that room was tough. The room containing the skulls and bones was simply unbearable. Prior to this, I had only seen skulls in my line of work, and trust me they were few.

"I came out of that room a sober man. I am a surgeon, I have seen patients die, but I had never seen such horrific deaths in my life. The reasons given for slaughtering nearly one million people in 100 days is unfathomable. As I am person who thrives on research I thought it wise to learn more about the genocide. So I visited a bookstore to buy some books on this subject. Ikirezi bookshop in Kigali had a lot of books on the subject. And to be honest I was initially looking for a book written by a Rwandan. I did find a few, but truthfully I didn't feel they were comprehensive enough, so I settled for one written by the French academic and historian Gerard Prunier. The book is *The Rwanda Crisis: History of a Genocide.*

"Now before I even share some insights from this book, I want to make reference to one of the reasons I've observed that has impeded development in some African countries, so add this to the points I mentioned above: many Africans fail to express their thoughts in writing or to document history. For some reason, they take delight in hiding information. I mentioned Harvard-educated adventurer Francis Tapon earlier; he once said that 'He could not imagine the Internet or Wikipedia being invented in Africa because generally Africans don't like to share knowledge.'

"Ouch, Ouch, Ouch Alex, that is a very harsh statement!"

"Well yes, but Abdul, how many of your friends regularly edit or contribute to Wikipedia? How many books on history, politics, business, science, have you read by African writers? How many biographies have you read that were written by an African? The majority of African countries gained independence over 40 years ago. So we can say that most African countries have had a president or ruler for that long. But the question is how many African Presidents have written autobiographies or books on any subject or have lived their lives in such a manner that others could write about them?

"Let's take a single country: the United States of America, for example. Out of the former U.S. Presidents since 1923, only George H.W. Bush has not written an autobiography. Even though George H.W. Bush hasn't written an autobiography, he has written a book containing some of his letters and other writings. However, many books have been written about him. Numerous politicians and business leaders in the U.S. have books written about them. So Abdul, you have to start writing your thoughts down and encourage your friends to do the same. Because collectively these thoughts can become books, which people will read and learn from."

"Alex, you have made a very important point. I will challenge myself to start writing a book now. I won't wait till I am President before I write a book."

"So as I was saying about Gerard Prunier's book, *The Rwanda Crisis: History of a Genocide,* from opening the first chapter, it was obvious why the genocide happened. Over 80 years before the genocide, the seeds of superiority were sewn among the Tutsis by the first Europeans who came to Rwanda. To quote Prunier, 'The Europeans were quite smitten with the Tutsi, whom they saw as definitely too fine to be Negroes. Since they were not only physically different from the Hutu but also socially superior, the racially-obsessed nineteenth-century Europeans started building a variety of hazardous hypotheses on their possible, probable, or as they soon became indubitable origins. The man who started it all was John Hanning Speke, the famous Nile explorer.'

Here are some other descriptions from the book:

'We can see Caucasian skulls and beautiful Greek profiles side by side with Semitic and even Jewish features, elegant golden-red beauties in the heart of Ruanda and Urundi ... The Bahima (a Tutsi clan) differ absolutely by the beauty of their features and their light colour from the Bantu agriculturalist of an inferior type. Tall and well proportioned, they have long thin noses, a wide brow and fine lips. They say they come from the North. Their intelligent and delicate appearance, their love of money, their capacity to adapt to any situation seem to indicate a Semitic origin.'

"The descriptions go on and on. I urge you to read this book, Abdul. But please be warned that this book contains some heartbreaking information."

"Then why should I read it Alex, if my heart will be broken?"

"Well I believe you should study history because it greatly helps to understand cultures and the evolution of thought over time. It is just like studying about the slave trade. Even though the stories are harrowing, you must understand your history. Actually when you were in Ghana did you ever visit Cape Coast Castle?"

"Oh yes I did. Seeing the dungeons that the slaves were kept in made me cry. And what amazed me was that on top of the dungeon, there was a church."

"Abdul, what I have come to understand about religion in my short life is that sometimes unscrupulous people who have the audacity to call themselves pastors, apostles or prophets take passages of scripture out of context and use them to manipulate or enslave others. Look, even Jesus in Matthew 7:15 warned us about false prophets. These are his exact words: 'Beware of false prophets, who come to you dressed as sheep, but inside they are devouring wolves.'

"Now back to my story about Rwanda. So yes, a mixture of racial prejudice, colonization, religion, chieftaincy, internal wars, and other factors contributed to the genocide of 1994, claiming the lives of nearly one million people in 100 days. Nothing happens in a vacuum. There are always underlying causes, though sometimes the causes are not clear. You have to dig deep to find them.

"The good news is that if you visit Rwanda today, you will see, feel, and experience a different story. A story not of hatred and anger but a story of hope, forgiveness, the spirit to rebuild, peace, stability and great leadership. Kigali is a clean city, a city where plastic bags are not welcome. On day three of my visit, I headed for Kigali's famous craft market, the Kimironko market. I wandered through the market talking to the market men and women, and then I bought a few souvenirs.

"Leaving the market I saw a local eatery, so I decided to go there to relax and eat. After ordering my food, a gentleman walked past me, so I said hello and introduced myself and asked him who he was. He said he was the manager of the restaurant. He asked if I was happy with their service. Then I asked him to sit down so we could chat. I then began asking him what he thought about his country and a host of other questions. His name was Innocent, and he had studied psychology in University, so he could speak fluent English. He told me he was working in the restaurant to acquire business knowledge and also save money to set up a business. I was impressed by his plan and tenacity.

"Innocent gave me so much history, and also spoke about the changes his country was undergoing. He said he was one of those who wanted Paul Kagame to remain in power. When I asked why, his response astounded me. Innocent apparently was a genocide survivor. During the genocide, he lost six siblings and his father. Abdul, goose bumps suddenly came over me. What!!! This is what he told me: 'Yes, I mean I lost 7 of my nuclear family members. It was only my Mum and I who escaped. This is one of the reasons I want the current President, Paul Kagame, to remain in power. Kagame has brought stability to us; he has brought security, freedom of movement, peace, better education, investors and many other things. Generally Kagame and his team are helping to create a positive business environment and name for Rwanda. We have also been able to move on from the genocide and are optimistic about our future.'

"Meeting Innocent was definitely one of my highlights in Rwanda.

"Now Abdul, the interesting thing about Paul Kagame remaining in power is that article 101 of the Rwandan constitution states that

'The President of the Republic is elected for a term of seven years renewable only once. Under no circumstances shall a person hold the office of President of Republic for more than two terms.'

"However, article 193 states that:

'The power to initiate amendment of the Constitution is vested concurrently in the President of the Republic upon the proposal of the Cabinet and each Chamber of Parliament upon a resolution passed by a two thirds majority vote of its members. The passage of a constitutional amendment requires a three-quarters majority vote of the members of each chamber of Parliament. However, if the constitutional amendment concerns the term of the President of the Republic or the system of democratic government based on political pluralism, or the constitutional regime established by this Constitution especially the republican form of the government or national sovereignty, the amendment must be passed by referendum, after adoption by each Chamber of Parliament. No amendment to this article is permitted.'

"So there you go, even though one clause says a President must leave after serving two seven-year terms in office, another says this can be changed by passing a referendum. And this is the clause Kagame supporters are banking on.

"Since talks began to amend the constitution in a referendum, some governments, especially in the West are touting Kagame as a dictator and a man hungry for power. They talk as if Kagame wants to remain in power by force. If the referendum is successful he will have to contest for election in 2017 like all the other candidates. If he wins that election then he will be president for a 3rd term. I find the outcry from some western countries hypocritical. I researched the number of terms a President can have, and in Europe alone I found that the German Chancellor has no term limit. That is why the current chancellor, Angela Merkel, whom I am a devotee of, was elected for a 3rd term in 2015. She can still be elected for a 4th term if her party wants her to remain their leader and if she wins the election. This is the same for our beloved country the United Kingdom. If this were not the case, Margaret Thatcher couldn't have been Prime Minister for 11 years. In Italy the Prime Minister can have an unlimited number of 5-year terms, in The Netherlands, Prime Ministers can have unlimited 4-year terms.

"Abdul, I definitely want you to visit Rwanda and see for yourself the progress they have made. Also study their constitution.

It is precise and easy to read. Even a 16-year-old can read and understand it. Learn from the leadership of Rwanda, I will suggest you meet some of them. When you do, ask them questions like why they are succeeding when some African countries are not. But on the subject of the constitutional amendment, let's leave Rwandan's to decide. I could go on and on about Rwanda. When I was in Rwanda one message I kept on hearing from the people was about the leadership of Paul Kagame. So my next lesson is about leadership, a subject very dear to my heart.

CHAPTER NINE

Lead by Example

"The quality of a leader is reflected in the standards they set for themselves."

— Ray Kroc

Leadership is a topic very dear to my heart, and for you it should be one you study on a daily basis—to help you become all that you were created to be. But even more so because of your aspirations to become Ghana's president. I have personally learnt principles of leadership from eminent teachers like Robin Sharma, John Maxwell, and Brian Tracy. However, today I will like to focus on leadership principles taught by one of my favourite teachers, Dr. Myles Munroe.

"My interest in Dr. Myles Munroe began fifteen years ago in the hot summer month of August. I was introduced to him by a friend. The first book I read, *Understanding Your Potential*, was an eye opener. After devouring this book in less than one week I was hungry for more so I read the sequels, *Releasing Your Potential and Maximizing Your Potential.* These books reiterated that I was sent here on earth to accomplish something specific. One simply had to discover what one's purpose was and pursue it. His style of writing was so simple and self-explanatory, but the principles he shared were profound.

"His simplicity in expressing ideas was such that even if a 16-year-old picked up any of his books on potential, he or she would understand it. I was hooked. His book *The Burden of Freedom: Discover the Keys to Your Individual and National Freedom* greatly impacted me. It explained that third-world countries are where they are because of the choices the people make. He made me understand that freedom in itself does not guarantee change or bring about development. Only a transformed mind brings about lasting change.

"To be honest Abdul, I have never felt oppressed and had no idea what people who were socio-economically or physically oppressed felt. After reading that book, I gained such an understanding on how to deal with the issues whenever I saw them. After I read that book I changed the style of our medical mission trips to some of these countries. Dr. Myles Munroe also had a marriage that inspired me. His deep commitment to his wife and family taught me that in today's world where some marriages are falling apart, one could still have a happy, meaningful, and fulfilling marriage.

"In the book *Understanding Love: Marriage, Still A Great Idea* he talked about the foundation of a happy marriage being the love God has for us; Agape Love and true friendship. Jean and I picked up so many principles that helped us to have a thriving marriage today. And what can I say about his books on leadership? *The Spirit of Leadership, The Power of Character in Leadership, and "Becoming a Leader"* all changed my way of thinking, a thousand times over. Dr. Munroe defines leadership as '*...the capacity to influence others through inspiration, motivated by a passion, generated* *by a vision, produced by a conviction and ignited by a purpose.'* I believe this definition captures what true leadership is.

"Here are 10 key principles on leadership I have learnt from Dr. Munroe:

1. Trapped in every follower is a hidden leader.

2. Every human was created to lead and dominate in an area of gifting.

3. You were born to lead but you must become a leader.

4. The purpose of true leadership is to reproduce leaders.

5. True leaders are confident in who they are so they are not afraid to help you become who you are. True leaders are secure.

6. Leadership is not about controlling others; true leadership is about serving others.

7. Leadership is not about power but about empowering others.

8. Leadership is not about manipulation but about inspiration.

9. Leadership is not about people; true leadership is about purpose.

10. Leadership is about self-discovery and then self-release. Leadership is not about activity.

"Abdul, I meditate on these teachings all the time. Every day I ask myself if I am cultivating leaders. I am challenged every day to lead effectively and bring out the leader in others.

"Dr. Munroe did not just teach, he lived by example. He stood for integrity and was a pillar of hope to many. One of the reasons why he represented hope was the fact that he was born to a poor family, the 6th child of 11. The family, though so large, lived in a two-bedroom wooden house in Bain Town, in Nassau, Bahamas. I am sure when you hear of the Bahamas, your thoughts go to the azure-blue sea and mega-resorts like The Atlantis, Paradise Island built by South African magnate Sol Kerzner.

"Well yes, but not everyone in the Bahamas lives a grand life. Dr. Munroe had such courage. Frankly his courage could be likened to the strongest hurricane ever recorded in history. Dr. Munroe spoke publicly on difficult subjects like racism, sexuality, moral decadence, and corruption, when others simply took flight at the mere thought of discussion.

"In his book *The Power of Character in Leadership: How Values, Morals, Ethics, and Principles Affect Leaders,* Dr. Munroe challenges the reader to have values and convictions, as these attributes are the foundation to a sustainable legacy, a life of tremendous impact. Unfortunately in our world today we see the opposite. "We tend to value talent over character; we value reputation over character and value position over character. A good character is one's personal security system. Once you have good character you have nothing to fear. Being disciplined, accountable, and putting God first are some ways to develop good character."

"In an address Abraham Lincoln delivered to aspiring lawyers in July 1850, he said *'There is a vague popular belief that lawyers are necessarily dishonest ... Let no young man, choosing the law for a calling, for a moment yield to this popular belief. Resolve to be honest at all events; and if, in your own judgment, you cannot be an honest lawyer, resolve to be honest without being a lawyer. Choose some other occupation, rather than one in the choosing of which you do, in advance, consent to be a knave.'*

"Abdul, please understand that living a life with such high standards is not easy. You will actually be tested day-to-day, so I implore you to pass the small tests that come your way. I call them small tests because of your level now. I can tell you for a fact that the older and more prosperous you are, the more tests you will face on these fronts. Just imagine living in your dream home, driving your dream car, having chauffeurs to take you to work and the children to school, having access to all the movers and shakers in your city and having a large income every month. With the freedom that will bring, you can suddenly feel invincible. It is my prayer that you will not succumb to these pressures especially as you aspire to be president.

"Out of the 69 books Dr. Myles Munroe wrote (and it seems like he wrote them more quickly than I could read them), I have read 22.

A day I will never forget is Monday 10th November 2014. I woke up to the tragic news of the passing of Dr. Munroe, his wife Ruth Munroe and seven others in a plane crash.

All the relevant media in the world carried his death and life story. From CNN, Reuters.com, The Associated Press, Forbes.com, Al Jazeera, thetimes.co.uk, ABC News, NBC News, CBN, KTN, Christianity Today, Citifmonline.com, the Washington Post, and numerous others. Immediately after the story broke, leaders from all walks of life began sending their condolences. My attention was particularly drawn to the statement made by the Prime Minister of The Bahamas, The Right Honourable Mr. Perry Christie.

Here is an excerpt: *'It is utterly impossible to measure the magnitude of Dr. Munroe's loss to The Bahamas and to the world. He was indisputably one of the most globally recognizable religious figures our nation has ever produced. His fame as an ambassador for the Christian ministry preceded him wherever in the world he travelled, whether in the Caribbean, North America, Asia, Europe or Africa. He was a towering force who earned the respect and admiration not only of Christian adherents but of secular leaders both here at home and around the world. Dr. Munroe was a man of immense charisma and persuasive appeal. Whether one agreed with him or not, there was never any question that Dr. Munroe was a man of deeply held principles who never hesitated to speak truth to power. He was regarded by a great many persons as the Conscience of The Nation. Certainly, he was among the most defining and influential spiritual leaders of the modern Bahamas and, I daresay, of the wider world of Christian evangelism as well. Although Dr. Munroe and I disagreed on some matters over the years, I regarded him as both a personal friend and spiritual mentor. I leaned on his counsel in a number of important matters, most recently in the consultations with religious leaders on the pending constitutional bills, a process in which he took an enthusiastic and constructive part, helping even to re-draft one of the bills that had met with a great deal of public controversy.'*

"What a testimony. Many more tributes poured in from both friends and those who opposed him. Would you believe that even President Barack Obama sent a tribute? These were Obama's words: *'Michelle and I were saddened to learn of Myles and Ruth's passing, and we extend our hearts' condolences as you mourn their loss. Leaders like Myles and Ruth teach us that we are our brothers' and our sisters' keepers and challenge us to practice what we believe through our deeds as well as our words.'*

"This acclaim is unusual Abdul, considering the fact that Dr. Myles Munroe was not a politician—he never ran for any office. He was an ordinary citizen who rose to prominence. Due to his influence and the exemplary life he lived, he was invited to address the nation's parliamentarians in 2012. It was one of his most heartfelt messages. Here are some of the statements he made:

'No law in our country should violate first of all natural law that God gave us in creation and then divine law that God gave us in his word. Politicians think about protecting their seats, leaders think about protecting the unborn. Politicians focus on power, leaders focus on empowering. I challenge all Parliamentarians and Senators today find a purpose more important than power. Find a national vision that is bigger than your political party. Find convictions that are more important than compromise. Find values that are more important than vacillation. Find passion that is more important than popularity. Find the faith that is more important than facts. May God bless you with wisdom and humility and patience and the spirit of servitude as you lead our nation. Take us from where we are to where God wants us to be. We trust you, we believe in you that's why we voted for you. Running a country is tough. I weep over you because it's a tough job.'

"After uttering the last statement, he started weeping. Abdul, I have to give you the video to watch. When you become President, organize a weekly learning session with your cabinet ministers and make sure you watch this video as well as other great speeches by outstanding politicians. Also watch the speech Dr. Kwame Nkrumah made during independence. Whenever you do, you will be reminded of the purpose behind why you were elected.

"Dr. Myles Munroe walked the talk. His funeral, though a private ceremony, was recognized by the State. On the day, various roads were closed and others diverted just to make room for the burial of this great man. Global leaders and politicians from around the world convened to bid him farewell. It was a befitting sendoff for Dr. Myles and his precious wife Ruth Munroe.

"Even though he is no longer with us, his teachings and the 69 books he wrote are here to guide us.

"Abdul, now close your eyes ... I have a present for you."

"What is it Alex?"

"Here you go: open the box."

"Oh Alex, I can't believe this; 12 books written by Dr. Munroe for me?"

"Yes, you deserve it. Your hunger and desire to bring about change is so strong that I am compelled to help you fulfill that dream. You know, this is what happens when you are hungry for change. Whenever one gets to that point, God just sends helpers our way. We are all instruments of help to others, so every single day you wake up ask yourself this, 'Have I helped all those I was assigned to today?' Asking this question every day will change your life. You will no longer see the people you meet as pests but rather as those you are assigned to help."

"Alex, I have thoroughly enjoyed today's lessons. Thanks so much for having faith in me and for spending so much time with me. All the four thousand characters in the Chinese language are not enough to let you know how much I appreciate you!"

"Abdul, are there four thousand characters in Mandarin?"

"Well, in actual fact they number in the tens of thousands; however, to gain functional literacy in written Mandarin, you will need to recognize four thousand characters."

"Wow, I never knew that!"

"Really, Alex, I thought you would know this."

"Well Abdul, this is one thing you have to understand too: that no matter what you know, there will still be many things you won't know. That's why it is important to learn from as many people as you can. Never assume that a child cannot teach you a thing or two. So I thank you for teaching me something new.

"Abdul, I am very tired now. I am looking forward to seeing Jean and the quads and getting into my rituals."

"Oh yes Alex, you mean your rituals of taking a shower, drinking lots of water, having dinner with the children, listening to Jean tell you all about her day and snuggling up next to her, right?"

"Spot on Abdul.

"Finally, my ride home will be in silence as I will be listening to some roof-raising music by *Israel* to recharge my batteries. It will be so loud that you will be able to hear it from my earpiece. Please bear with me. Pick me up at 9am; I will be in meetings for a large part of the day. We will then decide what we should do after."

"That's ok Alex. I totally understand."

"Abdul, our lesson tomorrow will be … well, you'll have to wait—it's a surprise."

CHAPTER TEN

A Woman Is Like
A Tea Bag

"A woman is like a tea bag—you can't tell how strong she is until you put her in hot water."

— Eleanor Roosevelt

"Abdul, let's start out our day by once again discussing important and influential women, and note the great benefits to all of society in having empowered women as models to emulate. Let's begin with someone quite contemporary:

"Zhang Xin, a woman of considerable substance, is a Chinese business mogul. She is the co-founder and CEO of SOHO China, the largest real estate developer in Beijing. She founded this dynamic company with her husband Pan Shiyi. Zhang Xin came from very humble beginnings. Born in Beijing in 1965, at the age of 14 she moved to Hong Kong with her mother. As they tried to make a living, life was pretty rough for them. Zhang Xin wanted to further her education abroad, so for five years she worked in various electronic and garment factories. She said, 'As a new immigrant to Hong Kong with no education, no background, who didn't even speak the local language or dialect Cantonese, it was just a hard way to live in Hong Kong.'

"When she saved enough money, she bought a ticket to London and paid to study English in a secretarial school. Through hard work and commitment, she won a scholarship gaining admission to study Economics at the University of Sussex. As she was a very bright student, she went on to pursue a master's degree. In 1992, Zhang graduated from Cambridge University with a masters degree in Development Economics. She worked in the investment banking sector with Barings PLC in Hong Kong, then Goldman Sachs in New York. After meeting her husband Pan Shiyi, she moved back to Beijing to set up SOHO China. Today *Forbes* estimates her net worth at $3.6 billion dollars.

"Consider the facts that Zhang Xin didn't attend school until she was a teenager and has been able to achieve all that she has, even though she is under 50—what an outstanding achievement!

"Abdul, I bet if you had met her as a teenager working in a factory you would not in your wildest dreams have thought that she would make such impact in the future. Zhang's story reminds me every day never to underestimate anyone. We are all created with enormous potential, so don't feel superior to your fellow human being.

"Thankfully, with successful women like Michelle Obama, the first lady of the United States, and Elizabeth Holmes, founder of the health technology firm Theranos, who is currently the youngest female self-made billionaire in the world, history has further proved that women are equally as intelligent, enterprising and capable as men.

"Abdul, the next person I am going to tell you about is one of my personal idols. Forgive me to use such a strong word. It's not that I worship her; I understand that God, the creator of the universe, is the only one who needs to be worshipped. I am simply in awe of this woman. She is a neo futuristic architect whose buildings adorn cities around the world. Her buildings are synonymous with curves and fluidity. From a distance the buildings she designs look so fluid that you won't think they could be built with glass, stone and steel—but they are. I am greatly keen to visit cities that have her signature work. Two I will visit in the future are Innsbruck in Austria and Zaragoza in Spain. I just want to see the Bergisel Ski Jump and the Bridge Pavilion."

"Who is this great woman you are just talking about, Alex. Please tell me who she is."

"Hang on a minute Abdul. Let me tell you more about her achievements. The famed Guangzhou Opera House in Guangzhou, China and the Sheikh Zayed Bridge in Abu Dhabi, United Arab Emirates are also among some of her projects.

"Her most recent project is a centre for studying Middle Eastern culture, at St. Antony's College in the University of Oxford, which was commissioned in May 2015. This contemporary building of steel and glass is meshed between two Victorian buildings, giving it a look like no other. This is what her architectural firm had to say about the building's style: 'Its design weaves through the restricted site at St. Antony's College to connect and incorporate the existing protected buildings and trees, while its stainless-steel facade softly reflects natural light to echo the building's context.'

"Oh Alex, my curiosity is getting the better of me. I am itching to know who this person is."

"Hold on Abdul, I will spill the beans after this last project. The Aquatic center she built for the London Olympics in 2012 is a feast to the eye. This state-of-the-art center contains three different-sized swimming pools. Jacques Rogge, the incumbent IOC President at the time, described the centre as a masterpiece.

"She was born in Bagdad in 1950, studied mathematics for her first degree at the American University of Beirut then moved to the Architectural Association School of Architecture in London. She has lectured at the Harvard Graduate school of Design and several other universities. She is currently the professor at the University of Applied Arts, Vienna. I am talking about no other than Dame Zaha Mohammed Hadid."

"Wow what an impressive woman she is."

"Now Abdul, Zaha Hadid was the first woman ever to win the famous Pritzker Architecture Prize. This award was bestowed upon her in 2004. You know, the Pritzker prize is often referred to as the Nobel Prize of Architecture—it is the highest honour an architect can be awarded. The likes of Sir Norman Foster of the UK, Oscar Niemeyer of Brazil, Rem Koolhaas of The Netherlands, and Ieoh Ming Pei of China are all Pritzker winners. By the way, since the Pritzker family established the prize in 1979, no African has ever won this prize.

"Let's brainstorm about this later and see how we can help change this. What immediately comes to mind is setting up a scholarship fund to enable Africans attend prestigious architectural schools."

"Yes Alex, I buy into this idea. One of my goals will be to organize a fundraiser for this cause. My continent needs this."

"It's been two hours already; shall we call it a day now and continue tomorrow?"

"No Alex, please go on."

"Well yes, I will give you a bit more for today, then we will reconvene soon for more."

"Alex, am I not seeing you tomorrow?"

"Unfortunately not. I will be giving a lecture at the Edinburgh Medical School."

"Can I pick you up from home and drop you off at the airport at least?"

"Well, you know that Gatwick is only 33 miles on the M25.

So it would be better if I drove and parked the car at the airport. I am going on the trip with Jean. We'll have breakfast at the Virgin Atlantic clubhouse, then catch our flight at 10am. The lecture is at 12 noon. After the lecture, we will have lunch, stroll around the harbor in the New Town and discover interesting byways and sights. We have been to Edinburgh many times but we always look forward to going back.

"Abdul, have you been to Edinburgh before?"

"No Alex, I haven't."

"My oh my. Edinburgh is a city you must visit before you die. Seeing the historic Edinburgh castle on a warm summer's night will make you fall in love. Even though the castle was built in the 12th century it is still in use today.

"When I went to Edinburgh the very first time, I was stunned to see the sheer number of well-preserved stone houses in the city. Due to this reason the New and Old Towns are UNESCO World Heritage Sites.

"The Old Town of Edinburgh was founded in the Middle Ages, and the New Town was developed in 1767–1890. They contrast the layout of settlements in the medieval and modern periods. The layout and architecture of the New town, designed by luminaries such as William Chambers and William Playfair, influenced European urban design in the 18th and 19th centuries.

"Another point of interest in the city is the University. Edinburgh University is the sixth-oldest University in the English-speaking world and has one of the leading medical schools in the world. This university has produced luminaries in science, the arts, politics and more. A few examples include the physicist James Clerk Maxwell, philosopher David Hume, mathematician Thomas Bayes, surgeon Joseph Lister, inventor Alexander Graham Bell, and the first president of Tanzania Julius Nyerere. Plus a host of famous authors such as Sir Arthur Conan Doyle, Robert Louis Stevenson,

J.M. Barrie and Sir Walter Scott. Twenty Nobel Prize winners are a product of this great institution.

"Going back to our trip, sometimes when we are going on a date or holiday we have a theme for the occasion. I don't mean a colour theme. It's usually something to stretch us a little, like talking to as many strangers as we can or giving a compliment to anyone who deserves one. Our theme tomorrow will be on 'Smiling.' We aim to smile at each other many times and also smile to every one we meet. We will then count how many times we have smiled and determine the winner. Whoever wins will be given a GBP100 voucher from Amazon to buy books. I like playing the smile game. The last time we played this game, Jean won. So this time around, I intend to beat her by one hundred smiles at least. Playing the smile game will really make you happy. Try it and you will be amazed."

"Alex, I will try it with Halima at the weekend and let you know the score."

"But before I concentrate on Edinburgh, let's discuss a few more individuals that have made a difference in the world; such examples are always inspiring, and show that people can make changes that affect many lives for the better.

"The former U.S. president Clinton and Hillary Clinton are a couple I do admire. They remind me that one can bounce back from a setback. They also remind me that two intelligent and ambitious people can marry and be successful. Even though Hillary didn't serve in any government capacity when Bill Clinton was president, she ran for office to become the Senator of New York and won, becoming the first female senator representing that state, a position she held for eight straight years. She then became the third female Secretary of State. Don't forget that Hillary Clinton is a well-educated woman. Her success in politics has little to do with the fact that she is married to a former president—her achievements to date are based on merit. She holds a law degree from the Yale Law School.

"The last woman I will talk about is someone I look forward to meeting. She is one of the most intelligent and courageous women in the world. In the last 10 years she has been ranked the most powerful woman in the world by *Forbes* magazine. It all began in 1954, when a child was born in Hamburg in West Germany to Herlind Jentzsch, an English and Latin teacher, and Horst Kasner, a theologian. Angela Dorothea Kasner was a very bright child. She learnt to speak Russian fluently and was interested in mathematics, a subject in which she won numerous awards. In 1973, she studied physics for her first degree at the University of Leipzig, graduating in 1978. She then pursued a doctorate degree and was awarded a doctorate in Physical Chemistry. Her thesis was on quantum chemistry.

"After the fall of the Berlin wall, Angela got involved in politics, joining the newly established Democratic Awakening party. This party eventually merged with the Christian Democratic Union. Angela stood for elections in 1990 and won. She became an MP and was appointed the minister for Women and Youth, a position she excelled in. In 1994 she was moved to the Ministry of Environment and Nuclear Safety and was the youngest cabinet minister under Helmut Kohl. For ten years, Angela worked tirelessly for her country and her party eventually winning the party nomination in 2005 to challenge Gerhard Schroder in the 2005 elections. Even though the CDU didn't win an outright majority in that election, a coalition was reached and Angela Merkel was chosen to become the German Chancellor. In March 2014, after being elected for a third term, Angela Merkel became the longest-serving head of state in the European Union. Under her leadership, Germany has grown into a European powerhouse.

"And her passion for football is undeniable. She attends games of the national team and when Germany won the 2014 world cup, she celebrated with them. Her husband Joachim Sauer, who is also a quantum chemist, is a pillar of strength for her. As the first female chancellor, Merkel proves that women can step up to the plate."

"You know, it's always hard saying bye to you. But I have to go now because the train to Guildford is approaching the platform. I will see you tomorrow."

"Bye bye, Alex."

CHAPTER ELEVEN

Who Will Mourn When You Are Gone

"True leaders don't invest in buildings. Jesus never built a building. True leaders invest in people. Why? Because success without a successor is failure. So your legacy should not be in buildings, programs or projects; your legacy must be in people."

— Dr. Myles Munroe

"Abdul, today, I have three very important things to share with you.

"The first thing I want to ask you is, what legacy would you like to leave behind?

"If you wake up every single day asking yourself this all-important question, you will start making choices consistent with the legacy you want to leave. If you would like to leave a legacy of kindness, you must start being kind to others. Another way of looking at this is asking yourself what you want people to say at your funeral. In some ways, you are preparing for your death by having lived the proper life.

"Now this habit shouldn't scare you at all. Rather, it will urge you to truly live. I started asking myself this all-important question when I turned thirty-eight years old and believe me, this has helped shape me into who I am today. At that age, I decided that at my funeral I wanted it said that:

I lived life to the fullest.
I forgave all those who offended me.
I was kind to everyone I met.
I brought joy everywhere I went.
I gave others the chance of a better life.
I touched thousands of hearts.
I made a difference.

"Because of this advance obituary I wrote, everything I do in life is guided by it. This way of thinking gives me perspective about any challenges I am facing. Because of this philosophy, I cannot be angry with everybody or anybody. I want it said at my funeral that I brought joy to everyone I came into contact with. I cannot be revengeful in life and expect to hear that I was forgiving. I cannot be stingy and expect to hear that I was kind-hearted.

"Think legacy every day, Abdul.

"Secondly, I want to introduce you to a man who shattered my beliefs about what is possible. A man who blew all my excuses away and made me realize that the only limitations we have are the limitations we place on ourselves. A man who infused me with so much faith, faith to believe that, 'All things are possible to them that believe.' This man is Erik Weihenmayer.

Erik was born in 1968 in Hightstown, New Jersey. His parents noticed defects in his eyes as a little boy. They took him to various eye specialists, who happened to all have different diagnoses of his ailment, but finally at the age of three, Erik was fortunate to have been sent to Retina Associates, the famous Boston eye clinic. There, Dr. Brockhurst diagnosed him as having retinoschisis, a very rare eye disease that would eventually cause blindness. Upon hearing this news, his parents were devastated. However, they were determined to give their son the best they could. Erik began kindergarten in a private school for the sighted, but he was given thick magnifying glasses that enabled him to read. Erik was raised as a 'normal' boy; his parents even gave him chores to perform at home. Instead of the usual bedtime stories parents read to their children, Erik's dad, a Princeton graduate and Marine Corps pilot, would read out loud his favourite poem, Don't Quit. Erik was taught how to ride a bicycle, play football and indulge in the activities a normal child would partake in.

But with each passing year, his eyesight grew worse until at 14 years old, he became completely blind. This was an extremely difficult time for the entire family and especially for Erik. Adjusting to blindness was a very difficult process. He still remained in his school, and a special teacher was assigned to him to teach him Braille and how to use a cane. Within months, Erik came to grips with his new life of blindness and was settling in rather well when the unthinkable happened. When he was 16 years old, his mother died suddenly in a car accident.

Erik was crushed. How could his mother die at a time in his life when things were taking a turn for the better? He grieved for a long time. In the spring after his mother's death, he was sent to a one-month summer camp for the blind in Boston, Massachusetts. That camp was life-changing, as he interacted with blind people who acted very normal. Some boys asked some of the girls there out on dates. He was taught how to handle his blindness, so blindness would not become disabling. He was taught to use systems to find things. For example, putting safety pins on different parts of pairs of socks to be able to identify them.

He was also taught how to hear the different sounds objects make in life situations. He learnt to swim and rock-climb, sports he would embrace much later in his life. Not long after the camp session, Erik received a guide dog called Wizard to help him move around. Wizard become his inseparable companion and enabled Erik to live a normal life. Through Erik's hard work, he gained admission to Boston College in 1987 and majored in English.

While in university, Erick begun experiencing severe pain in his left eye so went to see his specialist, Dr. Brockhurst. He was given the horrific news that his left eye would have to be removed and he would be fitted with a prosthetic eye. This prosthetic eye was made of a liquid paste that could be taken out, leaving a bulging hole in his eye socket. After realizing he had no choice, he obliged and thankfully the surgery was successful.

Some years later, he, his dad, and brother went on a holiday to Peru to hike the Inca trail. His dad, wanting him to enjoy the entire adventure, guided him on the trail, where he climbed mountains and ascended the 1,500 steps at Machu Picchu. This hiking adventure began a hiking tradition in the family, where they went trekking regularly and visited remote, ancient civilizations.

After graduating from college, Erik gained admission to pursue a Master's degree in Education. Before starting his courses, he wanted to work and he applied for summer jobs like washing dishes in a restaurant, but was turned down—not because he didn't qualify but because he was blind. This was a hard blow for Erik to swallow. As he later said, he learnt the lesson that 'People's perceptions of our limitations are more damaging than those limitations themselves.' After gaining his MA in Education, Erik was offered a job in Phoenix, Arizona at the prestigious County Day School. The 5th graders he taught opened a world of possibilities to him. The children became his eyes when he was in the classroom. They taught him many ways a blind person could effectively teach sighted children. At County Day School, Erik also fell in love with Ellen, a 6th-grade teacher.

While teaching in Arizona he used to go rock climbing with a friend Sam, and one day while climbing, Sam casually asked if they should consider climbing a bigger mountain like Mount Denali, which at 6,194 meters is the highest mountain in North America. They trained very hard for months on end and finally the day came when they flew to Anchorage in Alaska to climb Denali. After a grueling 19 days and challenges which nearly derailed them, they made it to the summit of Denali in June 1995.

Because Erik could not see, Sam said, 'Congratulations, you're standing on the top of North America.' Erik could not believe it because according to him, 'It seems strange that the last step felt no different from the thousands and thousands of previous steps I had taken in the last 19 days. It was just another step and I was there.'

Erik made news around the world when he summited Denali. He became an ambassador for the blind and attracted sponsors and received speaking engagements. Discovering his true potential and ability to do the impossible, Erik successfully climbed many more mountains. With such passion for mountain climbing, he left his teaching job and moved to the Rocky Mountains in Colorado, where he married his sweetheart Ellen.

Mountaineering became his life and in August 1997, he summited Mount Kilimanjaro, Africa's highest peak. His third mountain was

Mount Aconcagua in Argentina. He failed in his first attempt in December 1997 but succeeded the second time in January 1999. His fourth summit was Mount Vinson in Antarctica in January 2000. In May 2001, Erik made history by being the first blind man to summit Mount Everest. This achievement put him in the limelight and etched his name in the annals of great mountaineers.

His speaking engagements after Everest exploded. He began speaking to corporate America and was a speaker at international events. He was also interviewed by CNN and other leading networks. Despite his success, Erik did not settle but moved on to the sixth challenge, in June 2002 climbing the highest mountain in Europe, Mount Elbrus in Russia. In August 2008, Erik completed his seventh summit: the 4,845-meter Carstensz Pyramid in Indonesia, making history as the first blind man to summit all the seven highest peaks in the world. Erik still lives in Colorado with Ellen and his two children.

"You would think that after climbing all the mountains there were to climb, Erik would slow down. But no. He has ventured into skiing, kayaking, adventure racing, cycling, ice-climbing and flying.

"Now Abdul, think about this. If a blind man has achieved all these incredible feats, what is your excuse? What limiting lies are you holding on to? By the way, here is a copy of Erik's autobiography, *Touch the Top of the World: a Blind Man's Journey to Climb Further Than the Eye Can See*. Please read this book once every year, but most importantly, attend any of the conferences Erik speaks at if you can. I can assure you, your life will never be the same.

"And finally here are 12 books I have read recently which have expanded me in ways I can't explain.

1. *Stop Acting Rich and Start Living Like a Real Millionaire* – Thomas J. Stanley

2. *His Inventions So Fertile: A life of Christopher Wren* – Adrian Tinniswood

3. *Why Nations Fail: The Origins of Power, Prosperity, and Poverty* – Daron Acemoglu & James A. Robinson

4. *Africa Must Unite* - Dr Kwame Nkrumah

5. *Public-Private Partnerships: Principles of Policy & Finance* – E. R. Yescombe

6. *How Will You Measure Your Life?* – Clayton M. Christensen

7. *From Colony to Superpower: US Foreign Relations since 1776* – George C. Herring

8. *Best Served Cold: the Rise, Fall and Rise Again of Malcolm Walker* – Malcolm Walker

9. *Quiet: the Power of Introverts in a World That Can't Stop Talking* – Susan Cain

10. *Ultramarathon Man; Confessions of an All-Night Runner* – Dean Karnazes

11. *Riding the Storm: My Journey To The Brink And Back* – Duncan Bannatyne

12. *Neo-Colonialism: The Last Stage of Imperialism* – Dr Kwame Nkrumah

"These books, like those I've given you in the past, will move you forward in understanding. Abdul, you have been a dedicated student of mine for many years. But now it's your time. The student is also the teacher. Until we speak again, remember that I love you and believe in you. Go and do good, and live your best life."

Abdul looked at me with damp eyes and said, "Princess, this is what has happened to me in the last 25 years. I will introduce you to Alex so you can thank him for helping me get this far. Alex is currently in Antananarivo performing free medical surgeries to those who need it most. I will organize a meeting when he returns in a month."

I can't wait to meet Alex Bond.

So, Abdul's lesson is my lesson, and I think it's a lesson for all of us. Reach for the stars, and you will find your arms long enough to make the journey.

ABOUT THE AUTHOR

Princess Umul Hatiyya Ibrahim Mahama is a dreamer and a doer. She has a passion to Inspire and Challenge others to defy the status quo in order to fully express their talents and gifts. Due to this passion and success Princess was named in 2015 by ndoherty. com as one of The 100 people leading extraordinary lives. She is the author of *THE MAD DUCK: How to Live Your Best Life.*

Princess is a sought-after teacher and speaker. She speaks to business leaders, corporate organizations and institutions. Her insightful and thoroughly researched talks on Personal Development, Leadership, the Mindset and Business Strategy have gained her audience with organizations such as Vodafone, Barclays Bank, Stanbic Bank, and the University of Cape Coast, Faculty of Social Science among others. In 2014, Princess partnered with SPEC Consult Limited, an award winning Human Capacity Development Organization to deliver a month-long intensive training programme for graduates and future business leaders at the flagship Global Graduate Academy. In 2015 Princess was a speaker at TEDx Accra, a platform for achievers making waves in their areas of industry. Princess has been interviewed on radio, TV and various online platforms. Some include The Citi Breakfast show, The Super Morning show, CAN TV Malawi, joinupdots.com and the award winning Mo Abudu show.

Currently on a mission to set a record as "The first African to visit every country in the world," Princess to date has been to 50 countries on 5 continents. Some of these countries include Australia, Hong Kong, Iceland, Japan, Madagascar, New Zealand and Rwanda.

She is a mother of 6 energetic girls, and is a marathoner.

Princess resides in Accra with her family and blogs at *www.theglobetrottingprincess.com*

NOTES

NOTES

NOTES

NOTES

NOTES

NOTES

www.ingramcontent.com/pod-product-compliance
Lightning Source LLC
Chambersburg PA
CBHW051913170526
45168CB00001B/372